Essential
Comprehension Strategies
for the Intermediate Grades

Jerry Johns

Susan Lenski

Roberta Berglund

Kendall Hunt
publishing company
4050 Westmark Drive • P O Box 1840 • Dubuque IA 52004-1840

Book Team

Chairman and Chief Executive Officer   Mark C. Falb
President and Chief Operating Officer   Chad M. Chandlee
Vice President, Higher Education   David L. Tart
Director of Publishing Partnerships   Paul B. Carty
Editorial Manager   Georgia Botsford
Developmental Editor   Melissa Tittle
Vice President, Operations   Timothy J. Beitzel
Assistant Vice President, Production Services   Christine E. O'Brien
Senior Production Editor   Sheri Hosek
Permissions Editor   Caroline Kieler
Cover Designer   Mallory Blondin

Author Addresses for Correspondence and Workshops

Jerry Johns
Consultant in Reading
E-mail: *jjohns@niu.edu*
Fax: 815-899-3022

Susan Lenski
Professor
Portland State University
Graduate School of Education
615 SW Harrison
Portland, OR 97207-0751
E-mail: *sjlenski@pdx.edu*
503-725-5403

Roberta Berglund
Consultant in Reading/Language Arts
E-mail: *bberglund@rocketmail.com*

Ordering Information

Address: Kendall Hunt Publishing Company
4050 Westmark Drive
Dubuque, IA 52004
Telephone: 800-247-3458, ext. 4
Website: www.kendallhunt.com
Fax: 800-772-9165

Cover images © Shutterstock, Inc.

Preface and Overview

Who Will Use This Book?

We have written this practical and useful book for inservice and preservice teachers. The book is ideal for professional development in schools, districts, and other types of programs where the focus is on comprehension instruction in the intermediate grades. It will also be a helpful supplement in undergraduate and graduate reading and language arts classes, as well as in clinical courses where there is a desire to provide useful strategies that have wide applicability with narrative and informational text.

What Are Some of the Outstanding Qualities of This Book?

1. The book contains comprehension strategies that have utility in reading as well as other areas of the curriculum.
2. The strategies are presented with helpful headings that quickly indicate when, why, and how to use them. You can also see whether the strategy can be used with narrative text, informational text, or both.
3. The strategies are presented in an easy-to-follow, step-by-step manner.
4. Most of the strategies contain one or more examples.
5. One or more reproducible masters accompany all of the strategies.

What Grade Levels Do the Strategies Address?

The strategies in this book were specifically written for use in the intermediate grades. After reading about a strategy, it should be quite easy to determine how best to use it with students. You may want to adapt some of the strategies to accommodate your teaching style and your students' particular needs. For some readers, the strategies may be used with materials you read to students. You can then complete the strategy through shared reading and writing. Other students will be able, after appropriate instruction, to use the strategies independently.

What Insights Have Been Provided by Research?

Comprehension can be viewed as a deep understanding of text that requires skill, will, explicitness, strategy, and purpose (Calfee, 2009).

There is little doubt that teaching results in student learning. A persistent problem is that of teachers mentioning a skill or assigning a task without taking the time to teach it. Instruction that is characterized by clear explanation, modeling, and guided practice can increase student learning (Duffy, 2002, 2003). The National Reading Panel (2000) compiled a large volume that offers several strategies for effective comprehension instruction. According to Cunningham (2001), the comprehension section of the report is potentially valuable. Other major reviews (Israel & Duffy, 2009; Pearson & Fielding, 1991; Tierney & Cunningham, 1984) and related writings (Ogle & Blachowicz, 2002; Pressley, 2000, 2002, 2005; Rand Study Group, 2002) support the following areas for an instructional focus.

1. Teach students to be aware of their own comprehension. This strategy is often referred to as comprehension monitoring.
2. Have students work together. This strategy is called cooperative learning.

3. Have students make graphic summaries of what they read through the use of graphic and semantic organizers.

4. Teach story and text structures.

5. Help students learn to ask and answer questions.

6. Teach students to summarize what they read.

The strategies selected for this book will help you in the area of comprehension instruction. The key ingredients, however, are your actions as the teacher.

○ Take time to teach the strategies.

○ Tell students how the strategies will help them become better readers.

○ Model how the strategies are used.

○ Think aloud by describing what goes on in your mind as you are using the strategy.

○ Provide guided practice so students can learn how the strategy will help them understand the lesson or text.

○ Reinforce students' efforts.

○ Develop the strategies over time and remind students to use the strategies in a variety of contexts.

○ Help students reflect on the strategies and evaluate their usefulness in various contexts.

Finally, we want to stress again the critical importance of teaching the strategies. Many of the strategies can be embedded in oral reading you share with students (Scharlach, 2008). This means you can teach the strategies as students are in the process of becoming independent readers.

Is This Book Easy to Use?

Yes! The format and organization of this book make it very user friendly. We have also included a Quick Reference Guide inside the front cover so you can quickly locate the various strategies and consider their use. Note that the strategies are listed in alphabetical order. In addition, there are further breakdowns of the strategies on the back cover so you can quickly locate them.

Where Should I Begin?

Glance at the Quick Reference Guide inside the front cover. Scan the strategies and find a particular strategy that interests you. Turn to the page for that strategy. Suppose you select Character Four Square on page 15. Under the title, you will see headings that include four areas (see example below).

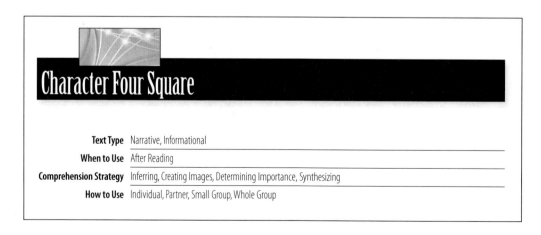

Character Four Square

Text Type	Narrative, Informational
When to Use	After Reading
Comprehension Strategy	Inferring, Creating Images, Determining Importance, Synthesizing
How to Use	Individual, Partner, Small Group, Whole Group

1. **TEXT TYPE** refers to the type of text materials with which the strategies can be used. Narrative text refers to stories; informational text generally refers to nonfiction materials. Character Four Square can be best used with both narrative and informational text.

2. **WHEN TO USE** tells you if you should use the strategy before, during, and/or after reading. Character Four Square is best used after reading.

3. **COMPREHENSION STRATEGY** is based on the work of Duke and Pearson (2002), Keene (2008), Keene and Zimmermann (1997), Pearson, Roehler, Dole, and Duffy (1992) and others who have conducted and reviewed the research in comprehension. These strategies help students become thoughtful, independent readers who are engaged in their reading and learning. The following are brief descriptions of the seven major strategies we use in this book.

    ○ *Monitoring Meaning*—Students who monitor meaning as they read know if the text makes sense to them. If not, they use fix-up strategies such as pausing, rereading, and/or discussing their understanding with others to help clarify the meaning.

    ○ *Using Prior Knowledge*—Students use their background knowledge before, during, and after reading to make sense of, and remember, new information. They assimilate new information into their background knowledge. This is sometimes referred to as using and developing their schema.

    ○ *Asking Questions*—Students generate questions before, during, and after reading. They use their questions to help them focus on and remember important ideas from the text.

    ○ *Inferring*—Students combine their prior knowledge with that which is read to create meaning that is not explicitly stated in the text. Readers who infer draw conclusions, make and revise predictions, use and interpret information from the text, make connections, answer questions, and make judgments about the reading.

    ○ *Creating Images*—Using all five senses and their emotions, students create images during and after reading. They may use their images to make connections, recall, and interpret details from the reading.

    ○ *Determining Importance*—As they read, students make decisions about what they believe is important in the text. These might be words, sentences, or main ideas developed from the reading. They then draw conclusions about the key ideas or major concepts contained in the text.

    ○ *Synthesizing*—Students put together information from the text, from other relevant sources, and their background knowledge to create understanding of what they have read. Students use text structures and text elements as they read to predict, confirm or reject ideas, assimilate thoughts and create overall meaning. "A synthesis is the sum of information from the text, other relevant texts, and the reader's background knowledge . . . produced in an original way" (Keene, 2008, p. 252).

    Character Four Square gives students an opportunity to use the processes of inferring, creating images, determining importance, and synthesizing.

4. **HOW TO USE** refers to whether the strategy is best used with individuals, partners, small groups, and/or whole groups. Character Four Square can be used with individuals, partners, small groups, and/or whole groups.

Below these headings are the words *Description, Teaching Goals Related to Learner Outcomes*, and *Procedure* (see page vi). There is a brief description of Character Four Square, three teaching goals, and a step-by-step procedure for using Character Four Square. We like to think of the numbered steps as a systematic lesson plan to help you present the strategy to your students. You should, of course, feel free to adapt the steps and examples to fit the needs of your students.

Character Four Square

Text Type	Narrative, Informational
When to Use	After Reading
Comprehension Strategy	Inferring, Creating Images, Determining Importance, Synthesizing
How to Use	Individual, Partner, Small Group, Whole Group

Description

Character Four Square is a strategy to help teach or review characterization in a story or selection. Students can make inferences to come up with some of the information requested. The information is then placed in four squares.

Teaching Goals Related to Learner Outcomes

1. To help students describe various aspects of a character in a reading selection.
2. To encourage students to select or suggest vocabulary that describes or portrays a character.
3. To have students create images that help identify a character's traits and feelings.

Procedure

1. Choose a book or story with a character (person or animal) that will be relatively easy for students to describe. Initially, use a short text with one main character to read to the entire class.
2. Display the reproducible on page 18 or draw a square with four quadrants on the board. Label them as shown in the example below.

Character's Name	Physical Description
Feelings	**Character Traits**

We often provide one or more *examples* (see example below) of how the strategy might be used in your curriculum. You may quickly be able to think of logical extensions to your lessons in a variety of areas.

Character Four Square

Character's Name	Physical Description
Lou Gehrig (Iron Horse)	strong but grew weaker
Feelings	**Character Traits**
felt good because he helped his family frustrated as he became weak thankful for what he was able to do	talented competent courageous modest shy

To make the strategy especially useful, one or more *reproducible masters* are included with all of the strategies. You have the publisher's permission to reproduce and use the masters with your students within the guidelines noted on the copyright page of this book. Now, it's time for you to use the strategies to help develop and enhance your students' comprehension.

References

Calfee, R. C. (2009). Preface. In S. E. Israel & G. G. Duffy (Eds.), *Handbook of research on reading comprehension* (pp. xi–xv). New York: Routledge.

Cunningham, J. W. (2001). The National Reading Panel Report (Essay Book Review). *Reading Research Quarterly, 36,* 326–335.

Duffy, G. G. (2002). The case for direct explanation of strategies. In C. C. Block & M. Pressley (Eds.), *Comprehension instruction: Research-based best practices* (pp. 28–41). New York: Guilford.

Duffy, G. G. (2003). *Explaining reading: A resource for teaching concepts, skills, and strategies.* New York: Guilford.

Duke, N. K., & Pearson, P. D. (2002). Effective practices for developing reading comprehension. In A. E. Farstrup & S. J. Samuels (Eds.), *What research has to say about reading instruction* (3rd ed.) (pp. 205–242). Newark, DE: International Reading Association.

Israel, S. E., & Duffy, G. G. (Eds.). (2009). *Handbook of research on reading comprehension.* New York: Routledge.

Keene, E. O. (2008). *To understand: New horizons in reading comprehension.* Portsmouth, NH: Heinemann.

Keene, E. O., & Zimmermann, S. (1997). *Mosaic of thought.* Portsmouth, NH: Heinemann.

National Reading Panel. (2000). *Teaching children to read: An evidence-based assessment of the scientific research literature on reading and its implications for reading instruction.* Washington, DC: National Institute for Child Health & Human Development.

Ogle, D., & Blachowicz, C. L. Z. (2002). Beyond literature circles: Helping students comprehend informational text. In C. C. Block & M. Pressley (Eds.), *Comprehension instruction: Research-based best practices* (pp. 259–274). New York: Guilford.

Pearson, P. D., & Fielding, L. (1991). Comprehension instruction. In R. Barr, M. L. Kamil, P. B. Mosenthal, & P. D. Pearson (Eds.), *Handbook of reading research* (Vol. II) (pp. 815–816). White Plains, NY: Longman.

Pearson, P. D., Roehler, L. R., Dole, J. A., & Duffy, G. G. (1992). Developing expertise in reading comprehension. In S. J. Samuels & A. E. Farstrup (Eds.), *What research has to say about reading instruction* (2nd ed.) (pp. 153–169). Newark, DE: International Reading Association.

Pressley, M. (2000). What should comprehension instruction be the instruction of? In M. L. Kamil, P. B. Mosenthal, P. D. Pearson, & R. Barr (Eds.), *Handbook of reading research* (Vol. III) (pp. 545–561). Mahwah, NJ: Erlbaum.

Pressley, M. (2002). Comprehension strategies instruction: A turn-of-the-century status report. In C. C. Block & M. Pressley (Eds.), *Comprehension instruction: Research-based best practices* (pp. 11–27). New York: Guilford.

Pressley, M. (2005). *Reading instruction that works: The case for balanced teaching* (3rd ed.). New York: Guilford.

Rand Study Group. (2002). *Reading for understanding: Toward an R&D program in reading comprehension.* Santa Monica, CA: Author.

Scharlach, T. D. (2008). START comprehending: Students and teachers actively reading text. *The Reading Teacher, 62,* 20–31.

Tierney, R. J., & Cunningham, J. W. (1984). Research on teaching reading comprehension. In P. D. Pearson, R. Barr, M. L. Kamil, & P. Mosenthal (Eds.), *Handbook of reading research* (Vol. I) (pp. 609–655). White Plains, NY: Longman.

Jerry Johns has been recognized as a distinguished teacher, writer, outstanding teacher educator, and popular professional development speaker for schools, school districts, and conferences. His more than 700 presentations have involved travel throughout the United States and 13 countries. He has taught students from kindergarten through graduate school and also served as a reading teacher. Professor Johns spent his career at Northern Illinois University. He was also a Visiting Professor at Western Washington University and the University of Victoria in British Columbia.

Professor Johns served in leadership positions at the local, state, national, and international levels. He has been president of the International Reading Association, the Illinois Reading Council, the Association of Literacy Educators and Researchers, and the Northern Illinois Reading Council. He also served on the Board of Directors for each of these organizations as well as the American Reading Forum. In addition, Dr. Johns has served on numerous committees of the International Reading Association and other professional organizations.

Dr. Johns has authored or coauthored nearly 300 articles, monographs, and research studies as well as numerous professional books. His *Basic Reading Inventory*, now in the tenth edition, is widely used in undergraduate and graduate classes as well as by practicing teachers. Among his more than 20 coauthored books to help teachers strengthen their reading instruction are *Improving Reading: Interventions, Strategies, and Resources, Strategies for Content Area Learning, Teaching Reading Pre-K–Grade 3, Spanish Reading Inventory, Comprehension and Vocabulary Strategies for the Elementary Grades,* and *Reading and Learning Strategies: Middle Grades through High School.* Professor Johns currently serves on the editorial advisory boards for *Reading Psychology* and the *Illinois Reading Council Journal.*

Dr. Johns has been the recipient of numerous awards for his contributions to the profession. The Illinois Reading Council honored him with the induction into the Reading Hall of Fame. Other recognitions include the Alpha Delta Literacy Award for Scholarship, Leadership, and Service to Adult Learners and the A.B. Herr Award for outstanding contributions to the field of reading. He also received the Outstanding Teacher Educator in Reading Award presented by the International Reading Association, the Champion for Children Award presented by the HOSTS Corporation, and the Laureate Award from the Association of Literacy Educators and Researchers for life-long contributors to the field of reading.

Susan Lenski is a Professor at Portland State University. Dr. Lenski has taught in public schools for 20 years. Her teaching experiences include working with children from kindergarten through high school. Dr. Lenski currently teaches graduate reading and language arts courses.

Professor Lenski has been recognized by several organizations for her commitment to education. Among her numerous awards, Dr. Lenski was presented with the Nila Banton Smith Award from the International Reading Association (IRA) for her work in integrating content area subjects with reading instruction in the secondary school. As an elementary school reading specialist, Dr. Lenski was instrumental in her school receiving an Exemplary Reading Program Award from the International Reading Association. She served on the Board of Directors of the IRA from 2004–2007.

Professor Lenski's research interests are in improving reading and writing instruction in elementary and secondary schools. She has conducted numerous inservice presentations and has presented at many state and national conferences. Dr. Lenski has written more than 60 articles for professional journals and 15 books.

 **Roberta (Bobbi) Berglund** has had a long and distinguished career in education. Her public school experience spans more than thirty years and includes serving as a classroom teacher, reading specialist, Title I Director, and district curriculum administrator. For several years, Dr. Berglund was a member of the reading faculty at the University of Wisconsin-Whitewater where she taught graduate and undergraduate reading courses and worked with student teachers. She has also taught graduate reading courses at several other colleges and universities including Northern Illinois University, Rockford College, National-Louis University, and Aurora University. Dr. Berglund has served as a consultant in the area of reading, working with school districts and cooperative education services in developing curriculum and assessments, conducting staff development, and guiding the selection of instructional materials. She is currently working with Response to Intervention initiatives as well as planning and implementing effective reading instruction for English Language Learners (ELLs) in the elementary grades. She recently received a grant to refine the use of evidence-based vocabulary and comprehension strategies to assist ELLs in accessing and reading informational text.

Dr. Berglund has received honors for outstanding service to several organizations and has been selected as a member of the Illinois Reading Council Hall of Fame. She was also honored with the Those Who Excel Award from the Illinois State Board of Education. She has served on several committees of the International Reading Association (IRA) including the Program Committees for the Annual Convention and the World Congress in Scotland. She has also chaired the Publications Committee which provided leadership for four professional journals, a newspaper, and the development of professional books. She provided leadership in the conceptualization and establishment of a free, internet-based source of high-quality practices and resources in reading and language arts instruction. Dr. Berglund has also served as the editor of a professional journal and has been on the editorial advisory boards for several others.

Dr. Berglund conducts workshops for teachers and administrators and has been invited to make presentations at state, national, and international conferences. She is the author of over fifty publications and is the author or coauthor of eleven professional books including *Strategies for Content Area Learning: Vocabulary, Comprehension, and Response* and *Comprehension and Vocabulary Strategies for the Elementary Grades*.

Anticipation/Reaction Guide

Text Type	Narrative, Informational
When to Use	Before Reading, During Reading, After Reading
Comprehension Strategy	Monitoring Meaning, Using Prior Knowledge, Asking Questions, Inferring, Determining Importance, Synthesizing
How to Use	Individual, Partner, Small Group, Whole Group

Description

Before students begin reading, they should activate their prior knowledge. A strategy that prompts students to think about the key concepts of a story or selection before they read is an Anticipation Guide (Herber, 1978). The key concepts can be facts that students will learn from reading, or they can be opinion statements. An Anticipation Guide can also be used after reading to confirm or alter students' ideas and is commonly called a Reaction Guide. This strategy, therefore, can help students make predictions before reading, and it can also provide a framework for checking the accuracy of the predictions during and after reading.

Teaching Goals Related to Learner Outcomes

1. To encourage students to make connections between their background knowledge and the content of a reading selection.
2. To encourage students to make predictions.
3. To help students establish purposes for reading.
4. To provide opportunities for students to revise their predictions during and after reading.

Procedure

1. Identify a selection which you want students to read. The text should contain facts that students could learn or key concepts from which students can develop opinions.
2. List the facts or the concepts that you want students to learn.
3. After you have identified terms and ideas, create sentences that could be answered with a "yes" or a "no." Do not write open-ended questions. For example, you should write, "A tropical rain forest has four layers," rather than asking, "How many layers are in a tropical rain forest?"
4. Duplicate a copy of the blank Anticipation/Reaction Guide reproducible on page 4. Write the sentences on the lines. A sample Anticipation/Reaction Guide for tropical rain forests is on the next page.

Anticipation/Reaction Guide

<u>Tropical Rain Forests by J. Hurwitz</u>
Title and Author or Topic

Directions:

Before reading or listening, decide whether you agree or disagree with each of these statements. Circle "yes" or "no." After reading think about whether you still agree or disagree or whether you want to change your mind. Circle "yes" or "no."

Before Reading			**After Reading**	
Yes	No	1. <u>Tropical rain forests cover ten to fifteen percent of the earth's land.</u>	Yes	No
Yes	No	2. <u>A few tropical rain forests are found in the United States.</u>	Yes	No
Yes	No	3. <u>Scientists say that a tropical rain forest has four layers.</u>	Yes	No
Yes	No	4. <u>People have begun to live in rain forests in the last twenty years.</u>	Yes	No
Yes	No	5. <u>Tropical rain forests have become threatened.</u>	Yes	No

5. Duplicate and distribute copies of your completed Anticipation/Reaction Guide to students. Tell students that you want to know what they think *before* reading the selection. Emphasize that you don't expect students to know the answers, but that you want them to make their best guesses about whether the statements are correct or incorrect.

6. Read one of the statements with students. Ask them to decide whether they think the answer is "yes" or "no." Tell students to circle the answer that they think is correct to the left of the statements. Encourage students to work independently.

7. Have students read the remaining statements or read them to the students. Tell students to respond to each statement with their best guess.

8. After students have finished, tell them to read or listen to the selection, paying special attention to the ideas presented in the Anticipation/Reaction Guide statements.

9. After students have read the selection or story, have them revisit the Anticipation/Reaction Guide by reacting to the statements once more. This time have students respond to the right of the statements. After reading, discuss the idea that readers can change their minds while reading by saying something like the following.

> When you read, you have some ideas before you begin, just like we did before we read the selection. In this case, some of you were wrong, and you learned something. Most of you thought that people have begun to live in rain forests during the last twenty years. After we read, we learned that native people have lived in rain forests for thousands of years. After reading, you need to think about what you have learned and whether you need to change your mind about something.

10. An Anticipation/Reaction Guide using opinions rather than factual statements can be found below.

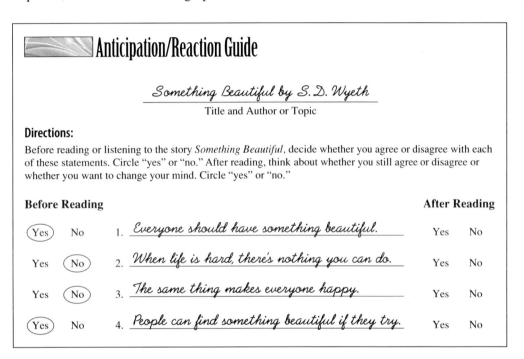

Anticipation/Reaction Guide

Something Beautiful by S. D. Wyeth
Title and Author or Topic

Directions:

Before reading or listening to the story *Something Beautiful*, decide whether you agree or disagree with each of these statements. Circle "yes" or "no." After reading, think about whether you still agree or disagree or whether you want to change your mind. Circle "yes" or "no."

Before Reading				After Reading	
(Yes)	No	1.	*Everyone should have something beautiful.*	Yes	No
Yes	(No)	2.	*When life is hard, there's nothing you can do.*	Yes	No
Yes	(No)	3.	*The same thing makes everyone happy.*	Yes	No
(Yes)	No	4.	*People can find something beautiful if they try.*	Yes	No

11. To use an Anticipation/Reaction Guide as a study tool, help students identify all the "yes" or "true" statements after reading. Then have students use the back side of their papers to rewrite all "no" or "false" statements to make them valid.

References

Herber, H. H. (1978). *Teaching reading in the content areas* (2nd ed.). Englewood Cliffs, NJ: Prentice-Hall.

Hurwitz, J. (2004). *Tropical rain forests*. Logan, IA: Perfection Learning.

Wyeth, S. D. (1998). *Something beautiful*. New York: Random House.

Name _____ Date _____

Anticipation/Reaction Guide

_____
Title and Author or Topic

Directions:

Before reading or listening, decide whether you agree or disagree with each of these statements. Circle "yes" or "no." After reading think about whether you still agree or disagree or whether you want to change your mind. Circle "yes" or "no."

Before Reading   **After Reading**

Yes   No   1. _____   Yes   No

                   _____

Yes   No   2. _____   Yes   No

                   _____

Yes   No   3. _____   Yes   No

                   _____

Yes   No   4. _____   Yes   No

                   _____

Yes   No   5. _____   Yes   No

                   _____

Yes   No   6. _____   Yes   No

                   _____

Name _____ Date _____

Anticipation Guide

_____
Title and Author or Topic

Directions:

Before you read or listen to a selection, decide if you agree or disagree with the statements written below. Circle "Agree" or "Disagree."

Agree   Disagree   1. _____

_____

Agree   Disagree   2. _____

_____

Agree   Disagree   3. _____

_____

Agree   Disagree   4. _____

_____

Agree   Disagree   5. _____

_____

Agree   Disagree   6. _____

_____

Agree   Disagree   7. _____

_____

Agree   Disagree   8. _____

_____

Agree   Disagree   9. _____

_____

Jerry Johns, Susan Lenski, & Roberta Berglund. _Essential Comprehension Strategies for the Intermediate Grades._ Copyright © 2011 by Kendall Hunt Publishing Company (1-800-247-3458, ext. 4). May be reproduced for noncommercial educational purposes within the guidelines on the copyright page. www.kendallhunt.com/readingresources

Name _____ Date _____

Reaction Guide

_____
Title and Author or Topic

Directions:

After you read or listen to a selection, decide whether you agree or disagree with the statements written below. Circle the word that fits your choice and explain why you feel as you do.

1. _____ Agree   Disagree

   _____

   Why? _____

   _____

2. _____ Agree   Disagree

   _____

   Why? _____

   _____

3. _____ Agree   Disagree

   _____

   Why? _____

   _____

4. _____ Agree   Disagree

   _____

   Why? _____

   _____

5. _____ Agree   Disagree

   _____

   Why? _____

   _____

Jerry Johns, Susan Lenski, & Roberta Berglund. _Essential Comprehension Strategies for the Intermediate Grades_. Copyright © 2011 by Kendall Hunt Publishing Company (1-800-247-3458, ext. 4). May be reproduced for noncommercial educational purposes within the guidelines on the copyright page. www.kendallhunt.com/readingresources

Bookmark Strategy Prompts

Text Type	Narrative, Informational
When to Use	During Reading
Comprehension Strategy	Monitoring Meaning, Using Prior Knowledge, Asking Questions, Inferring, Creating Images, Determining Importance, Synthesizing
How to Use	Individual, Small Group, Whole Group

Description

After decoding and comprehension strategies have been taught to students, there is a continuing need to give them opportunities to practice the strategies during reading. Some students may not remember the strategies or realize when a particular strategy may be useful. To help overcome these concerns, different Bookmark Strategy Prompts are provided for your use. These prompts will help students monitor their comprehension, something that should be fostered in comprehension instruction (Baker & Beall, 2009).

Teaching Goals Related to Learner Outcomes

1. To help students develop independence in monitoring their reading.
2. To encourage students to use a variety of strategies during reading.
3. To help students decode unknown words and comprehend reading selections.
4. To provide support for students as they use reading strategies independently.

Procedure

1. Review the Bookmark Strategy Prompts on page 9 and duplicate those that are most appropriate for your students. You can also create your own prompts. The bookmarks can be duplicated on card stock, laminated for durability, and cut apart for student use.
2. Be sure that you teach the various strategies on a particular bookmark before using the Bookmark Strategy Prompts. You can focus on a single strategy initially and then add additional strategies in subsequent lessons. General guidelines for teaching each strategy are listed below.
    - Create an awareness of the strategy. Help students understand how learning and using the strategy will make them better readers.
    - Define or explain the strategy using terminology that students will understand.
    - Model the strategy with instructional materials in your classroom. One way to model is to think aloud as you process the information (Wilhelm, 2001).
    - Provide students practice in the use of the strategy through the use of interesting and appropriate materials.
    - Encourage students to use the strategy as they engage in a wide variety of reading situations. The Bookmark Strategy Prompts are very useful reminders of strategies that can be used.

3. Use the bookmarks with the whole group, smaller groups who read at approximately the same level, groups who may need to learn or practice a particular strategy, or with individuals.

References

Baker, L., & Beall, L. C. (2009). Metacognitive processes and reading comprehension. In S. E. Israel and G. G. Duffy (Eds.), *Handbook of research on reading comprehension* (pp. 373–388). New York: Routledge.

Wilhelm, J. D. (2001). *Improving comprehension with think-aloud strategies.* New York: Scholastic.

What can I do to understand what I read?

1. Make a prediction and check to see if I am right.

2. Try to make a picture in my head.

3. Look at pictures in the book.

4. Think about what is happening.

5. Look for words I know.

6. Look at word bits and parts.

7. Fix my mistakes.

8. Read ahead.

9. Read it again to myself.

10. Read it again aloud.

11. Remember what happened first, next, and last.

12. Tell what it is about in a sentence.

13. Think, "Does this make sense?"

Jerry Johns, Susan Lenski, & Roberta Berglund. *Essential Comprehension Strategies for the Intermediate Grades*. Copyright © 2011 by Kendall Hunt Publishing Company. May be reproduced for noncommercial educational purposes.

Reading Strategies I Have Used

___ Use What I Already Know

p. _____

___ Monitoring Understanding

p. _____

___ Ask Questions

p. _____

___ Create Images

p. _____

___ Infer

p. _____

___ Determine Importance

p. _____

___ Summarize/ Synthesize

p. _____

Jerry Johns, Susan Lenski, & Roberta Berglund. *Essential Comprehension Strategies for the Intermediate Grades*. Copyright © 2011 by Kendall Hunt Publishing Company. May be reproduced for noncommercial educational purposes.

Good Readers

Make Predictions about what will be in the text.

I'm guessing that _____

I think this _____

Make Connections between the text, their lives, the world, and other books.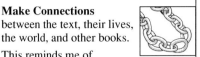

This reminds me of _____

This is like _____

Ask Questions of the author, of themselves, and of the text.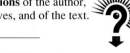

I wonder _____

What if _____

Make Pictures in Their Minds as they read and change them as they get new information.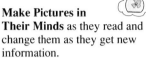

In my head I can see _____

I imagine _____

Determine Important Information by figuring out what ideas are most important to the meaning.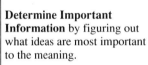

I think this is mostly about _____

Make Inferences by using what is known and clues in the text to make judgments or to predict.

Now I think _____

I think the author means _____

Synthesize by combining new information and what is known to get a new idea or interpretation.

Now I understand why _____

My new thinking is _____

I used to think _____; now I think _____

Use Fix Up Strategies by reading that part again, reading ahead, adjusting reading speed, or asking for help.

This is not making sense _____

This doesn't connect to _____

Jerry Johns, Susan Lenski, & Roberta Berglund. *Essential Comprehension Strategies for the Intermediate Grades*. Copyright © 2011 by Kendall Hunt Publishing Company. May be reproduced for noncommercial educational purposes.

Character Feelings

Text Type	Narrative, Informational
When to Use	After Reading
Comprehension Strategy	Inferring, Creating Images, Determining Importance, Synthesizing
How to Use	Individual, Small Group, Whole Group

Description

Character Feelings, based on Johns and Berglund (2011) and Johns and Lenski (2010), can be used with fictional characters, real people, or biographical sketches. Students' identification of the feelings should be based on an analysis of the printed material. Students should also provide evidence for their decisions. Small and whole group discussions can be used to help students share reasons for their choices and evaluate the choices offered by other students.

Teaching Goals Related to Learner Outcomes

1. To help students identify a character's feelings using stated and implied information in a reading selection.
2. To encourage students to understand and visualize how a character might feel.

Procedure

1. Identify a particular narrative or informational selection that can be read with or to students. When doing this activity for the first time, you may want to choose a selection that has only one main character. You may want to provide either a personal copy of the selection for students or use a large copy with the entire class. Subsequent selections can be read independently.

2. Draw or show a picture of a smiley face. Ask students what a smiley face represents. They may say happiness or joy. Accept any reasonable answer and write the word(s) on the board.

3. Ask students to think of any faces they can make that would show how a person might feel. Call on a student to show his or her face to the class without saying anything. Have other students "guess" what face is being presented and write appropriate feeling words on the board. Then encourage students to share other feelings that are internal; they may not be revealed by facial expressions. Add these words to the list and clarify as necessary.

4. Have students read the selection or read the selection to them. After reading the selection, have students write or circle the words they think represent the feelings of the character. This can be done on the reproducible master on page 13 or on the board.

5. If the reading selection has several characters, you might also have students discuss the feelings of those characters.

**Essential Comprehension
Strategies
Decal # 371**

6. In subsequent lessons, expand the feelings fictional characters or real people can have and keep a list where students can consult it. Possible feelings that might be included are listed below.

excited	bored	surprised	silly
angry	confused	confident	nervous

7. Be sure to take sufficient time to discuss and help students understand particular emotions that may be unknown or vague.

8. Expand Character Feelings by having students identify feelings at the beginning, middle, or end of the story or selection (see reproducible on page 14). Students can also explain why the character's feelings changed or did not change. Below is an example based on *Who Belongs Here?* (Knight, 2003). Nary is a young boy fleeing war-torn Cambodia for the safety of the United States.

Changes in Character Feelings

Directions:
Choose a character in the story. Write the name of the first character on the line. Then think of feelings the character had at the beginning, middle, and end of the story. Write the feelings on the line. Explain why the character's feelings changed or did not change.

Nary
Character

sad/confused	*nervous/happy*	*secure*
Beginning of Story	Middle of Story	End of Story

Why did the character's feelings change?
Nary moved to a different part of the world.

Why did the character's feelings change?
Nary felt safe in his new place.

References

Johns, J. L., & Berglund, R. L. (2011). *Strategies for content area learning* (3rd ed.). Dubuque, IA: Kendall Hunt.

Johns, J. L., & Lenski, S. D. (2010). *Improving reading: Interventions, strategies and resources* (5th ed.). Dubuque, IA: Kendall Hunt.

Knight, M. B. (2003). *Who belongs here? An American story.* Gardiner, ME: Tilbury House.

Character Feelings

Directions:

Choose some characters in the story. Write the name of a character on each line. Circle the word in the box that tells how the character in the story felt or add words to describe how the character felt. Then explain why the character had that feeling.

_____
Character

Happy	Scared	Sad	Very Sad	Mad
_____			_____	

Why? _____

_____

_____

_____
Character

Happy	Scared	Sad	Very Sad	Mad
_____			_____	

Why? _____

_____

_____

_____
Character

Happy	Scared	Sad	Very Sad	Mad
_____			_____	

Why? _____

_____

_____

Changes in Character Feelings

Directions:

Choose a character in the story. Write the name of the first character on the line. Then think of feelings the character had at the beginning, middle, and end of the story. Write the feelings on the line. Explain why the character's feelings changed or did not change.

Character

_____

Beginning of Story	Middle of Story	End of Story

Why did the character's feelings change?

_____
_____
_____
_____

Why did the character's feelings change?

_____
_____
_____
_____

Character Four Square

Text Type	Narrative, Informational
When to Use	After Reading
Comprehension Strategy	Inferring, Creating Images, Determining Importance, Synthesizing
How to Use	Individual, Partner, Small Group, Whole Group

Description

Character Four Square is a strategy to help teach or review characterization in a story or selection. Students can make inferences to come up with some of the information requested. The information is then placed in four squares.

Teaching Goals Related to Learner Outcomes

1. To help students describe various aspects of a character in a reading selection.
2. To encourage students to select or suggest vocabulary that describes or portrays a character.
3. To have students create images that help identify a character's traits and feelings.

Procedure

1. Choose a book or story with a character (person or animal) that will be relatively easy for students to describe. Initially, use a short text with one main character to read to the entire class.
2. Display the reproducible on page 18 or draw a square with four quadrants on the board. Label them as shown in the example below.

Character's Name	**Physical Description**
Feelings	**Character Traits**

You might also want each student to complete a Character Four Square. Students can share their square with a partner or in small groups. Then have the whole group share feelings and traits while you list them on the board. Clarify as needed and note that some words, like *nervous*, can be both a feeling and a trait.

3. Before reading the story, it may be helpful to relate aspects of Character Four Square to yourself. You may want to invite students to share their ideas, so you can help them distinguish between feelings and traits.

4. Explain the procedure and the words in each quadrant. You might say the following.

> Look at the words in each of these squares. Let's talk about what these words mean. Stories have characters. They can be people or animals. After I read *Lou Gehrig: The Luckiest Man* (Adler, 2001), I will write the name of Lou Gehrig here. [Point to the appropriate square.] In the next square, I will list words that tell what the character looks like—what I would see if I looked with my eyes. As I read, I think of some feelings the character may have. I'll want to list those here.

5. After reading the selection, invite students to decide which character to write in the top left quadrant. Then add any physical description students can remember. You may want to read certain parts of the selection again to help students recall descriptions, feelings, and traits. Systematically complete the Character Four Square, offering clarification as needed. Below is a completed example for *Lou Gehrig: The Luckiest Man*.

Character Four Square	
Character's Name Lou Gehrig (Iron Horse)	**Physical Description** strong but grew weaker
Feelings felt good because he helped his family frustrated as he became weak thankful for what he was able to do	**Character Traits** talented competent courageous modest shy

6. Be sure to help students understand that most feelings and traits must be inferred from what the characters say and do. Below is an example.

> Mr. Adams: When we list feelings and traits, the author may not actually say the words. We have to infer or guess what the author might have in mind from the story. Who has an idea for a word that describes Lou Gehrig's character? Be sure and tell why you think so. What is your evidence?

> Cherrith: I think he was talented because he was so successful playing ball.

> Corey: He was also modest. The story said he was modest. I think that was true because he didn't brag about his accomplishments.

> Max: I think he was courageous when he got ALS, a deadly disease that affects the central nervous system.

> Josh: I agree. He was also modest when he was honored by the Yankees.

> Mr. Adams: You have shared some appropriate traits for Lou Gehrig. I especially liked how you used your ideas along with the story to come up with words. Do you also think he was competent?

7. If the story or selection has other characters, they may be discussed using another Character Four Square.

8. When students understand the strategy, have them work in small groups, with partners, or individually. Some students may prefer to draw pictures of the character and some of the feelings and descriptions. Reproducible masters can be found on pages 18 and 19.

Reference

Adler, D. A. (2001). *Lou Gehrig: The luckiest man.* Boston: Houghton Mifflin.

Character Four Square

Character's Name	Physical Description
Feelings	**Character Traits**

Jerry Johns, Susan Lenski, & Roberta Berglund. *Essential Comprehension Strategies for the Intermediate Grades.* Copyright © 2011 by Kendall Hunt Publishing Company (1-800-247-3458, ext. 4). May be reproduced for noncommercial educational purposes within the guidelines on the copyright page. www.kendallhunt.com/readingresources

Character Four Square

My character's name	Words that tell how my character looks
Feelings my character shows or has	**A drawing of my character showing traits**

Character Traits

Text Type	Narrative, Informational
When to Use	After Reading
Comprehension Strategy	Using Prior Knowledge, Inferring, Creating Images, Determining Importance, Synthesizing
How to Use	Individual, Partner, Small Group, Whole Group

Description

Character Traits, based on Johns and Berglund (2011) and Johns and Lenski (2010), is similar to Character Feelings on page 11 except the focus is on the *traits* of fictional characters or real people. Students are encouraged to analyze the materials read, identify specific traits of the character or person, and provide reasons for the traits they select. In some instances, the traits may be a word or words from the text. In other instances, students will need to infer traits using information in the text and their background knowledge. _____

Teaching Goals Related to Learner Outcomes

1. To help students use stated and implied information in a selection to identify the traits of a character or person.

2. To encourage students to justify reasons for the traits they have chosen.

3. To help students expand the repertoire of words they use for character traits.

Procedure

1. Write the word *traits* on the board and invite students to share their ideas about the word's meaning. Guide students as necessary to arrive at a meaning that is student-friendly. Some key ideas are listed below.

   special quality of a person or character
   a characteristic someone has

   You might want to tell students that character traits are descriptive adjectives (define if necessary) that tell the specific qualities a character has. Then select a story likely known by most students (*The Three Little Pigs*) and have them share qualities and characteristics along with their reasons for choosing specific words. Guide students as necessary.

2. Invite students to share some traits people or characters can have. You might begin with a famous person such as Abraham Lincoln and ask a volunteer to share a trait. Write the traits on the board (e.g., honest, hard working, serious, sense of humor). If necessary, clarify the difference between *traits* and *feelings*. Be sure that students provide reasons or evidence for the traits suggested. In many cases, the traits identified will be based on the actions of the person or character.

3. Continue by asking students to think of some of the characters in books, selections, and other materials that they have read. Have students identify the character and traits associated with that character. One student, for example, may identify the trait *hard-working* with Paul Bunyan. Another student may say that Thomas Edison was *creative* and *intelligent*. A third student may suggest that Mother Teresa is characterized by the traits of being *humble* and *compassionate*.

4. Help students see that a trait is often inferred from a series of things the character or person does or says. At other times, the trait may be stated in the text.

5. Duplicate sufficient copies of the Character Traits reproducible on page 24 so each student has one.

6. Model how to use the reproducible by selecting a person or character familiar to students. Below is a sample related to Thomas Edison.

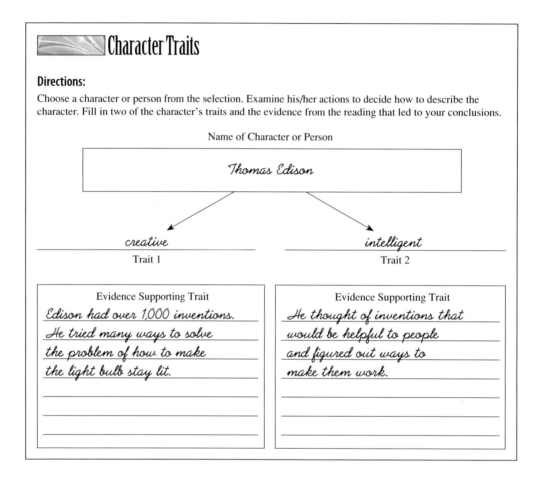

7. Answer any questions and then direct students to the selection to be read. Have students read the selection and, as they read, encourage them to think about traits related to a particular character or person and reasons why a particular trait was chosen. It is often helpful for students to write down specific actions that can help reveal one or more character traits. If the selection has more than one character, invite students to choose one.

8. After students have completed their Character Traits sheet, have them get together with a partner or in small groups and share their findings. If multiple characters are in the selection, group students having the same character.

9. When small group sharing is completed, have students share with the entire group, stressing reasons why a particular trait was chosen. Help students realize that some traits may actually be mentioned in the selection while other traits may need to be inferred from the character's actions.

10. In subsequent lessons, expand students' vocabulary related to character traits by selecting words from the list on page 23. Take time to teach selected words and relate them to characters or people studied.

11. Students might want to draw pictures of selected characters and people and list specific traits along with reasons why specific traits were chosen.

Examples of Character Traits

able	curious	good	mischievous	serious
active	dainty	graceful	miserable	sharp
adventurous	dangerous	grateful	mysterious	short
affectionate	daring	greedy	naughty	shy
afraid	dark	grouchy	neat	silly
alert	decisive	grumpy	nervous	simple
ambitious	demanding	guilty	nice	skillful
angry	dependable	happy	noisy	sly
annoyed	depressed	hard-working	obedient	smart
anxious	determined	harsh	obnoxious	sneaky
apologetic	disagreeable	hateful	old	sorry
arrogant	discouraged	healthy	patriotic	spoiled
attentive	dishonest	helpful	peaceful	stingy
average	disrespectful	honest	picky	strange
bad	doubtful	hopeful	pitiful	strict
blue	dreamer	hopeless	plain	strong
bold	dull	humble	pleasant	stubborn
bored	dutiful	humorous	pleasing	studious
bossy	eager	ignorant	polite	successful
brainy	easygoing	imaginative	poor	sweet
brave	efficient	impatient	popular	talented
bright	embarrassed	impolite	positive	thankful
brilliant	encouraging	impulsive	precise	thoughtful
busy	energetic	inconsiderate	prim	thoughtless
calm	evil	independent	proper	thrilling
careful	excited	industrious	proud	timid
careless	expert	innocent	quick	tired
cautious	fair	intelligent	quiet	tireless
charming	faithful	inventive	rational	tolerant
cheerful	fancy	jealous	reliable	touchy
childish	fearless	joyful	religious	trusting
clever	fierce	keen	reserved	trustworthy
clumsy	fighter	kindly	respectful	unfriendly
coarse	foolish	lazy	responsible	unhappy
compassionate	fortunate	leader	restless	unselfish
conceited	foul	light	rich	upset
concerned	fresh	light-hearted	rough	useful
confident	friendly	lively	rowdy	warm
confused	frustrated	lonely	rude	weak
considerate	fun	lovable	sad	wicked
cooperative	fun-loving	loving	safe	wild
courageous	funny	loyal	satisfied	wise
cowardly	gentle	lucky	scared	witty
creative	giving	mature	secretive	worried
cross	glamorous	mean	self-confident	wrong
cruel	gloomy	messy	selfish	young

Adapted from Gardner, T. (2010). *Becoming a character: Adjectives, character traits, and perspective.*
http://www.readwritethink.org/classroom-resources/lesson-plans/become-character-adjectives-character-168.html

Character Traits

Directions:

Choose a character or person from the selection. Examine his/her actions to decide how to describe the character. Fill in two of the character's traits and the evidence from the reading that led to your conclusions.

Name of Character or Person

[box]

Trait 1 _____   Trait 2 _____

Evidence Supporting Trait	Evidence Supporting Trait
_____	_____
_____	_____
_____	_____
_____	_____
_____	_____
_____	_____
_____	_____
_____	_____
_____	_____
_____	_____
_____	_____

Connections Chart

Text Type	Narrative, Informational
When to Use	During Reading, After Reading
Comprehension Strategy	Using Prior Knowledge, Inferring, Creating Images, Synthesizing
How to Use	Individual, Partner, Small Group, Whole Group

Description

A Connections Chart helps students make connections during and after reading. Students make connections to themselves, other texts, and the world at large. Making connections is an internal reading process used by good readers that can be demonstrated to novice readers (Hartman, 1995).

Teaching Goals Related to Learner Outcomes

1. To help students see ways to connect current reading to their lives, other texts, and the world.
2. To help students identify the part of the text that triggered their connections.
3. To provide students with practice in making connections during and after reading.

Procedure

1. Tell students that good readers make connections to their lives, other books they have read or heard, and other things they know. Explain that readers often make general connections as they read and after they have finished reading.

2. Tell students that readers should be able to identify the words in the story that helped them think of something else. Tell students something like the following.

   When you read, you probably make many connections. You might not even be aware of these connections until you think about them. Today, I'd like you to be intentional about the connections you make by identifying the words in the story that trigger connections. When you identify words, phrases, and passages that help you think of other things, you will be able to explain how you made the connection and give evidence to support your ideas.

3. Provide an example of a book you've read, the words that triggered your memory, and the things that came to your mind as in the example that follows.

   Last night I read the picture book *Henry Works* by D. B. Johnson (2004). It's a fictional story about one day in the life of a well-known writer, Henry David Thoreau. As I read the book, I noticed several things in the story that reminded me of personal experiences and things I know. While I was reading the first page of *Henry Works*, I noticed that Henry decided to walk to work. Although I live too far away to be able to walk to work right now, I know many people who like to walk to work. I pictured my friend, Swapna, walking to work as I read.

   Later in the book, Henry met several friends on the way to work. This part reminded me of taking a walk down the sidewalk in my neighborhood and talking to my friends.

As Henry was walking to work, it started to rain. He kept walking. That reminded me of the many times I walk in the rain.

At the end of the story, Henry's friend asked him if he went to work. Henry said he was working; he was writing a book. Then Henry went into his cabin and wrote, "Today I took a walk in the woods." This reminded me of *Walden*, a book by Thoreau and also books I've read about writers.

Thinking about the book as a whole, I thought about Henry walking and then writing. It reminded me of what I've learned about prewriting.

4. Explain to students that sometimes a specific word will trigger a connection and that other times larger parts of the story will help them think of connections. Ask students if they have questions or need clarification about the strategy. Answer questions and provide clarifications if needed.

5. Tell students that you have a reproducible to help you organize your thinking. Show them how you would put the information from *Henry Works* on the reproducible as in the example below.

Name **Example**

Date

Title **Henry Works**

Connections Chart

This text said . . .	This reminded me of . . .
Henry walked to work.	Swapna walking to work.
Henry met friends along the way.	Walking in my neighborhood.
Henry walked in the rain.	I walk in the rain a lot.
Henry was writing a book.	Walden

Books about writers. |
| Henry was thinking as he walked. | What I've learned about prewriting. |

---

6. Provide students with a book that is easy for them to read that lends itself to making connections. Have students read the book independently, in partners, or read the book to the class. Ask students to write down connections as they read using the reproducible on page 28.

7. Tell students that sometimes they will find making connections easy and other times it will be difficult. Ask students to rate how easy it was to make connections to their book by raising from one to five fingers, with one being very difficult and five being very easy. If the book was difficult for many of the students to make connections, provide students with additional support or use a different book.

8. Have students share their connections and write them on the board along with the part of the book that triggered the connection. Draw students' attention to the variety of connections that are made from the same section of the book.

9. Some groups of students will need no further demonstration of this strategy, and others will need you to explain how to make connections from text more than once. After students are comfortable making connections, tell students that there are three broad categories of connections: self, text, and the world.

10. Select another text that students will be able to read and have them make connections as they have done in the past.

11. Draw three columns on the board with the headings: self, text, and world. Have students share their connections and place them in one of the categories. Provide students with support as needed.

12. Show students the reproducible on page 29. Have students who are able to identify the different types of connections use this reproducible when they read. You might use the reproducible on page 28 for English language learners and students who are not yet able to identify the different categories of connections.

13. Have students use the reproducible several times until you are confident that they make connections during and after reading. Tell students that readers make these connections automatically and that once they show proficiency making connections, they will be expected to do so automatically.

14. Incorporate the strategy of making connections during classroom discussions and writing activities. Have students tell the connections they've made as well as what triggered the connection.

References

Hartman, D. K. (1995). Eight readers reading: The intertextual links of proficient readers reading multiple passages. *Reading Research Quarterly, 30,* 520–561.

Johnson, D. B. (2004). *Henry works.* Boston: Houghton Mifflin.

Name _____ Date _____

Title _____

Connections Chart

The text said . . .	This reminded me of . . .

Name _____

Date _____

Title _____

Connections Chart

Directions:

Fill in the "From the Reading" box for each connection. Then fill in the connections boxes that fit the connections you make.

From the Reading	Connections to Self	Connections to Text	Connections to the World

Directed Reading-Thinking Activity (DR-TA)
Directed Listening-Thinking Activity (DL-TA)

Text Type	Narrative
When to Use	Before Reading, During Reading, After Reading
Comprehension Strategy	Monitoring Meaning, Using Prior Knowledge, Asking Questions, Inferring
How to Use	Small Group

Description

The Directed Reading-Thinking Activity (DR-TA) (Stauffer, 1975) and its companion strategy, the Directed Listening-Thinking Activity (DL-TA) (Richek, 1987), help students become critical readers or listeners as they make and check predictions about the content of a text. While the DR-TA and DL-TA can be used with informational text, they are most often introduced and used with narrative text. The DR-TA and DL-TA help students set purposes for reading or listening, understand information, actively read or listen to a text, and check the accuracy of predictions made about its content.

Teaching Goals Related to Learner Outcomes

1. To help students become actively involved in reading or listening to a selection.
2. To encourage students to make predictions and ask questions prior to and during reading or listening.
3. To encourage students to set purposes for reading or listening.

Procedure

1. Select a book or story that can elicit rich predictions. A selection with a well-defined plot and events, as well as a surprise ending, are often useful in introducing this strategy.
2. Prior to introducing the book or story to students, choose a small number of stopping points in the text. These points could be related to major events in the story or those that will encourage reflection and conjecture about the meaning of the text. Plan to display the questions on page 33.
3. Invite students to look at the title or cover of the reading material and answer the following question.

   What do you think this book (or story) is going to be about?

   Provide opportunities for several students to respond. You may want to record their predictions on the board, on chart paper, or on the reproducible on page 34. As students offer predictions, follow each by asking, "Why?" or "What makes you think so?" Allow several students to make predictions and explain their thinking.

4. In order to involve all students in making predictions and setting purposes for reading or listening, ask those students who have not actively made predictions to raise their hands indicating which prediction they agree with. You might say the following.

   Anita, we have three predictions written on the board. Which one do you think is the best prediction for what our story is going to be about?

5. In some situations you might use the following options. Read each prediction aloud and have students raise their hands to indicate their choice. For younger students, after three or four predictions are given, have the students who contributed the predictions move to different corners of the room. Have the remaining students go and stand with the person whose prediction they agree with. Repeat this process after each stopping point in the selection.

6. When several predictions have been made, ask students to read or listen until a predetermined stopping point in the text has been reached. Then ask students to reconsider their predictions.

   Were your predictions correct? Why or why not? [Invite several students to explain their thinking.]

7. When several of the predictions have been discussed, ask students if they wish to change their predictions and/or to make new ones. Again, ask them to explain their reasoning.

8. Continue with the prediction, read (or listen), and prove cycle until enough information has been presented for the ideas to begin to converge. At this point, finish the story.

9. At the completion of the story, follow up with reading (or listening) response activities, word study, meaningful rereading, or concept development: students may also write a summary individually or with a partner. Reproducible masters on pages 33–34 are for use in a reading or listening center in the classroom.

References

Richek, M. A. (1987). DR-TA: 5 variations that facilitate independence in reading narratives. *Journal of Reading, 30,* 632–636.

Stauffer, R. E. (1975). *Directing the reading–thinking process.* New York: Harper & Row.

It is important to keep thinking as you read or listen. Remember to ask yourself these questions.

What is this going to be about?

What makes me think so?

What do I already know?

Was I right? Why or why not?

How could I change my ideas to match what I know so far?

What will happen next?

What makes me think so?

Name _____ Date _____

Title _____

Thinking about My Reading or Listening

Directions:

Before you read or listen, make a prediction about what will happen. Use the title, illustrations or what you already know to make your prediction. Explain why you think as you do. After reading or listening, evaluate your prediction and make a new one, if necessary.

My prediction _____

_____

Why I think so _____

_____

READ or LISTEN

What happened? _____

_____

Now I think _____

_____

Why I think so _____

_____

READ or LISTEN

What happened? _____

_____

Now I think _____

_____

Why I think so _____

_____

READ or LISTEN

What happened? _____

_____

Now I think _____

_____

Why I think so _____

_____

Jerry Johns, Susan Lenski, & Roberta Berglund. *Essential Comprehension Strategies for the Intermediate Grades.* Copyright © 2011 by Kendall Hunt Publishing Company (1-800-247-3458, ext. 4). May be reproduced for noncommercial educational purposes within the guidelines on the copyright page. www.kendallhunt.com/readingresources

Inference Chart

Text Type	Narrative, Informational
When to Use	During Reading, After Reading
Comprehension Strategy	Using Prior Knowledge, Inferring
How to Use	Individual, Partner, Small Group, Whole Group

Description

Helping students understand and use inferences is the foundation of comprehension. Making inferences involves using background knowledge and clues in the text to come up with ideas that are not explicitly stated (Harvey & Goudvis, 2007). For students with little experience in making inferences, graphic organizers can assist them in developing the ability to infer.

Teaching Goals Related to Learner Outcomes

1. To help students make inferences from the details or clues in texts.

2. To help students connect their background knowledge with textual clues to understand ideas not explicitly stated in the text.

3. To provide students with practice in using a graphic organizer to help them make inferences.

Procedure

1. Tell students that they will be practicing a strategy called inferring. Write the term "inference" on the board. Explain to students that learning to infer will help them with remembering and understanding what they read.

2. Explain to students that authors don't always write everything down in "black and white." They expect readers to "read between the lines" to determine the meaning. To be a successful reader, it is important to read what the author has written and also look for clues to additional ideas the author may be trying to convey. Using what we know as well as what the author tells us helps us to infer or figure out the author's meaning.

3. Ask students to remember and discuss times when they had to "read between the lines." You might use the following examples to see if students can make inferences using the information in the sentence as well as their background knowledge to determine what the sentence is about. You could say the following.

   I would like to demonstrate for you how easy it is to make inferences. It is something we do all of the time, whether we are reading, listening, or talking to someone. I am going to read some sentences to you. Each one only tells a part of a bigger story. Use your background knowledge as well as what the author tells you to determine what is happening. If you know, then you have made an inference.

   ○ She opened her gifts after she blew out the candles.

Students will most likely know immediately that the sentence describes a birthday party. Point out to students that the author did not explicitly state that the sentence was about a birthday party. Students were able to infer that by using what the author wrote as well as information in their heads from experiences they have had at birthday parties.

4. Continue practice in making inferences using the following sentences.
   ○ She told her teacher that she had forgotten to set her alarm clock the night before.
   ○ First, they bought the tickets, then they stopped for popcorn.

   Encourage students to use one of the following stems when sharing their inferences:
   ○ My guess is . . .
   ○ Perhaps . . .
   ○ Maybe . . .
   ○ It could mean . . .
   ○ I think . . .
   ○ I infer . . .

5. After students have successfully shared their inferences from one or two of the sentences, demonstrate using one of the Inference Chart reproducibles on pages 37–39. Duplicate and distribute the Inference Chart on page 37 to each student. Tell students that you will use the Inference Chart together using the following sentence: The yard was covered with leaves and branches.

6. Have students write the given sentence in the first box of the top row of the Inference Chart.

7. Ask students to write one of their personal experiences in the next column that relates to the idea in the sentence.

8. Finally, have students write their inference in the final box of the chart. Encourage them to use an inference stem to begin their sentence.

9. Have students discuss their inferences and any questions they may have.

10. Repeat the procedure using the following sentence: Today we are cleaning out our desks, and then we will take everything home.

11. When you are sure that students understand how to use Inference Charts, have them practice independently using a short text where several inferences can be made.

12. Remind students that when they read a book or story, they need to use the details and clues in the text as well as their background knowledge to make inferences. When they do this, they will have an easier time understanding and remembering what they have read.

Reference

Harvey, S., & Goudvis, A. (2007). *Strategies that work: Teaching comprehension for understanding and engagement* (2nd ed.). York, ME: Stenhouse.

Name _____ Date _____

Title _____

Inference Chart

Clues or Details from the Reading	My Experiences	My Inference

Name _____ Date _____

Title _____

Inference Chart

Clues from the Reading	My Life	What I Think
_____ _____ _____	_____ _____ _____	_____ _____ _____
_____ _____ _____	_____ _____ _____	_____ _____ _____
_____ _____ _____	_____ _____ _____	_____ _____ _____

Making Inferences
Reading Between the Lines

Question: (from the reading, our group, or my teacher)

_____

_____

_____

_____

What I know from the *reading*:

_____
_____
_____
_____
_____

What I know from my *brain*:

_____
_____
_____
_____
_____

My Inference
(be sure to use at least one "because")

_____
_____
_____
_____
_____
_____
_____

It Says—I Say—And So

Text Type	Narrative, Informational
When to Use	During Reading, After Reading
Comprehension Strategy	Using Prior Knowledge, Inferring, Creating Images, Synthesizing
How to Use	Individual, Partner, Small Group, Whole Group

Description

The strategy It Says—I Say—And So helps students develop an interpretation of the text using evidence from the text and their own background knowledge. Beers (2003) suggests that students use this graphic organizer as they read the text to construct meaning.

Teaching Goals Related to Learner Outcomes

1. To help students use their prior knowledge and evidence from the text to make inferences.
2. To help students develop ways to build comprehension.
3. To provide students with practice in making inferences during and after reading.

Procedure

1. Tell students that they can develop their comprehension by thinking about what the text says, what they think based on their experiences, and their interpretation. Remind students that applying their own knowledge to a text is an important way to develop meaning.

2. Duplicate and distribute to students the It Says—I Say—And So reproducible from page 43. Tell students that this graphic organizer will help them think through the steps of the strategy.

3. Demonstrate the strategy It Says—I Say—And So by using an unfamiliar text such as *I Am an American: A True Story of Japanese Internment* (Stanley, 1994). Have students read a portion of the book independently. Demonstrate how to use the strategy by saying something like the following.

    The book talks about Pearl Harbor and the beginning of WWII and what happened to the Japanese living in America. The book describes what happened to Hachizo, Tsuru, and Shiro Nomura, a Japanese family. The parents immigrated to America, but Shiro was born in America and was a citizen. I am going to write down my ideas on the It Says—I Say—And So sheet.

4. Write down several facts from the text, what you thought about when you read it, and what it could mean as in the example that follows.

It Says	I Say	And So
Shiro was an American citizen who was placed in an internment camp during WWII.	This happened to one of my friend's grandparents. They had to go away and live in an army barrack.	The things I learn about history have happened to real people. When I read about Shiro, I can remember that he really lived at the same time as my own grandparents.
The farmers in some areas were concerned about the Japanese taking over the areas.	I know one of the orchards near me was originally owned by Japanese. I heard that they left during WWII, but I didn't think about internment.	Sometimes things happen that seem unjust such as when the family near me had to give up their orchard.

5. Have students read several more pages from the book and write down something they remember. Then have students write down what they were thinking about when they read in that section. Finally, have them think about what it means and write it in the last column.

6. Give students the opportunity to share their ideas in small groups. Have individual students share some of their ideas. Discuss how students can make generalizations from the text and their own ideas.

7. Demonstrate It Says—I Say—And So several times until students are able to complete it independently. Then have students use the strategy as they read.

8. Tell students that good readers use information from the text along with their own ideas to construct meaning and make interpretations.

References

Beers, K. (2003). *When kids can't read: What teachers can do*. Portsmouth, NH: Heinemann.

Stanley, J. (1994). *I am an American: A true story of Japanese internment*. New York: Scholastic.

Name _____ Date _____

Title _____

It Says	I Say	And So

Knowledge Rating

Text Type	Narrative, Informational
When to Use	Before Reading, After Reading
Comprehension Strategy	Using Prior Knowledge, Asking Questions
How to Use	Individual

Description

Knowledge Rating (Blachowicz, 1986; Blachowicz & Fisher, 2006) is a strategy that helps students become aware of the words in a text prior to reading it. The strategy helps students activate their prior knowledge about a topic and encourages them to develop mental questions and predictions about what is to be read. Students can also return to the Knowledge Rating sheet after reading and, using a different color pen or pencil, rate their knowledge of the words again.

Teaching Goals Related to Learner Outcomes

1. To create student interest in reading a selection.
2. To help students preview new and familiar vocabulary in a reading selection or unit of study.
3. To help students activate prior knowledge and develop a purpose for reading.

Procedure

1. Carefully select key vocabulary words from the selection to be read. Mix words that are new to the students with those that may be familiar to them.
2. Write these words on the reproducible on page 47, duplicate it, and distribute it to students.
3. Model how to use the sheet by saying something like what follows.

   This week we are going to be learning about *tropical rain forests*. The sheet contains some of the words that will be in our reading. It helps to think about what we know about some of the words in our text before we read. This helps us to be better readers. Look at the words from the text. Let's see how well we think we know these words before we read. [Explain each of the four categories and then have students put a check (✓) in the column that matches their knowledge.]

4. Help students realize that there is a range of knowledge for the first word by asking several students where they placed a check. Stress that different ratings are expected prior to reading the text.
5. Go to the next word and invite students to indicate their familiarity with the word. Invite a student to explain why he or she marked the word in a particular column.
6. When students appear to be comfortable with the Rate Your Knowledge grid, have students complete the grid independently. A sample completed grid is shown on page 46.

Rate Your Knowledge

Directions:

1. Rate in pencil before reading.
2. Read.
3. Rate again in pen or marker.

Vocabulary Word	4 I Can Define It.	3 I Can Use It in a Sentence.	2 I Have Heard of It.	1 I Have No Idea.
1. biomes				✓
2. region		✓		
3. tropical		✓		
4. ecosystems			✓	
5. climate	✓			
6. equator	✓			
7. underbrush	✓			
8. latitude			✓	
9.				
10.				
11.				
12.				

What new words did you learn today?

_____

_____

7. Finally, invite students to make predictions about the content of the lesson. After the lesson, the words can be revisited to assess knowledge gained about the words.

8. Additional reproducibles can be found on pages 48–49.

References

Blachowicz, C. L. Z. (1986). Making connections: Alternatives to the vocabulary notebook. *Journal of Reading, 29*, 643–649.

Blachowicz, C., & Fisher, P. (2006). *Teaching vocabulary in all classrooms* (3rd ed.). Upper Saddle River, NJ: Merrill Prentice Hall.

Rate Your Knowledge

Directions:

1. Rate in pencil before reading.
2. Read.
3. Rate again in pen or marker.

Vocabulary Word	4 I Can Define It.	3 I Can Use It in a Sentence.	2 I Have Heard of It.	1 I Have No Idea.
1.				
2.				
3.				
4.				
5.				
6.				
7.				
8.				
9.				
10.				
11.				
12.				

What new words did you learn today?

_____

_____

Name _____ Date _____

How Well Do I Know These Words?

Directions:

Here are some words from your reading. Before you read, put an "x" in the box that tells how well you think you know each word.

Word	1 Know It Well	2 Think I Know It	3 Don't Know It

Based on Blachowicz, C. L. Z. (1986). Making connections: Alternatives to the vocabulary notebook. *Journal of Reading, 29*, 643–649 and Blachowicz, C., & Fisher, P. (2006). *Teaching vocabulary in all classrooms* (3rd ed.). Upper Saddle River, NJ: Merrill Prentice Hall.

Name _____ Date _____

Knowledge Rating Before and After Reading

Directions:

Use these symbols: + = I know it. – = I don't know it. ? = I'm not sure.

Word	Before Reading Do I Know the Word?	After Reading Do I Know the Word?	After Discussion Do I Know the Word?	Meaning The Meaning or Definition of the Word

Jerry Johns, Susan Lenski, & Roberta Berglund. *Essential Comprehension Strategies for the Intermediate Grades*. Copyright © 2011 by Kendall Hunt Publishing Company (1-800-247-3458, ext. 4). May be reproduced for noncommercial educational purposes within the guidelines on the copyright page. www.kendallhunt.com/readingresources

K-W-L

Text Type	Narrative, Informational
When to Use	Before Reading, During Reading, After Reading
Comprehension Strategy	Monitoring Meaning, Using Prior Knowledge, Asking Questions, Determining Importance
How to Use	Individual, Partner, Small Group, Whole Group

Description

K-W-L (Ogle, 1986, 2002) is a strategy that provides readers with a framework for constructing meaning from text. Readers activate their prior knowledge through brainstorming (What I *K*now), define their purposes for reading by generating questions (What I *W*ant to Find Out), and monitor their reading by confirming their prior knowledge or extending their learning (What I *L*earned). The strategy can be used as a way of having the entire class brainstorm what they know about a topic before launching an investigation as well as a means of recording their learning once information is read or shared. Adaptations of K-W-L encourage students to identify possible sources of information and categorize the information. Students are also invited to identify additional questions following the reading. These questions can stimulate further research and inquiry.

Teaching Goals Related to Learner Outcomes

1. To help students build interest in and knowledge about a topic or unit of study.
2. To help students activate prior knowledge and establish purposes for reading.
3. To encourage students to monitor their reading.
4. To help students evaluate their prior knowledge.

Procedure

1. Display a K-W-L chart. Provide copies of the chart for each student, if you wish, using the reproducible on page 54.
2. Select a key concept from the topic being studied. For example, the topic being studied is the human body, and the key concept is the skeletal system. Brainstorm with students what they know about the concept. Record the information as it is shared under the heading, What I Know (or What I Want to Know). Encourage students to offer sources for the information shared. It may come from their personal experience, another person, technology, or reading.
3. After the brainstorming is complete, say the following to your students.

   Let's look at the information we think we know about our skeletal system. Do some of the ideas fit together? What categories of information might we be looking for as we read?
4. If students have difficulty clustering the brainstormed ideas into categories, you might say the following.

   I think one category of information might be the parts of the skeleton. Another one might be what different kinds of bones we have. Can you think of others?

5. As students discuss the information they think they know about a topic, questions arise, especially if there is disagreement about some of the information shared. For example, some students may think that some people are double jointed. Other students may believe differently. This leads to the next step in the K-W-L procedure, What I Want to Know. You need to help students develop questions about the topic, especially if there are gaps in the knowledge that students have shared or if there are inconsistencies or contradictions.

6. Record questions on the K-W-L chart that is visible to the class and encourage students to write down their questions on their personal K-W-L charts. This step helps students set purposes for their reading.

7. Following the reading, direct students to record what they learned under the L section of the chart (What I Learned). If there are still questions that were unanswered in the reading, you may wish to create a fourth column, What I Still Need to Learn, and explore with students how they might investigate these questions.

References

Ogle, D. M. (1986). K-W-L: A teaching model that develops active reading of expository text. *The Reading Teacher, 39,* 564–570.

Ogle, D. M. (2002). *Coming together as readers.* Arlington Heights, IL: Skylight.

 **K-W-L**

The Skeletal System

Topic

What I **Know**	What I **Want** to Know	What I **Learned**
Our skeleton is made up of bones. Bones give our body shape. Some bones we know: skull, back bone, ribs, thigh, arm, finger, toes, leg, hip. I once had a broken arm. Some people are double jointed.	How many bones do we have? How are bones held together? What are the parts of each bone? What are the purposes of bones?	We have 206 bones. Ligaments hold the bones together at a joint. The long leg bone has tough tissue on the outside, compact bone, and marrow. Bones are alive and growing. People are not double jointed. Their ligaments that hold their joints together are looser. The difference between a ball-and-socket joint and a hinge joint.

I Expect to Find Information in These Categories

A. Skeleton parts

B. Kinds of bones

C. Parts of bones

D.

Name _____ Date _____

K-W-L

_____
Topic

What I **Know**	What I **Want** to Know	What I **Learned**

I Expect to Find Information in These Categories

A. _____

B. _____

C. _____

D. _____

K-W-L-S-H

Topic _____

What We **Know**	What We **Want** to Find Out	What We **Learned**/ **Still** Need to **Learn**	**How** Can We Learn More?

Categories of Information We Expect to Use

A. _____ E. _____

B. _____ F. _____

C. _____ G. _____

D. _____ H. _____

Jerry Johns, Susan Lenski, & Roberta Berglund. *Essential Comprehension Strategies for the Intermediate Grades*. Copyright © 2011 by Kendall Hunt Publishing Company (1-800-247-3458, ext. 4). May be reproduced for noncommercial educational purposes within the guidelines on the copyright page. www.kendallhunt.com/readingresources

Name _____ Date _____

K-W-H-L-S Chart

Topic _____

Know What I Know	**Want** What I Want to Know	**How** How I Can Find What I Want to Know

Jerry Johns, Susan Lenski, & Roberta Berglund. *Essential Comprehension Strategies for the Intermediate Grades.* Copyright © 2011 by Kendall Hunt Publishing Company (1-800-247-3458, ext. 4). May be reproduced for noncommercial educational purposes within the guidelines on the copyright page. www.kendallhunt.com/readingresources

(continued)

Name _____ Date _____

Learn What I Learned	Still What I Still Want to Know

Jerry Johns, Susan Lenski, & Roberta Berglund. *Essential Comprehension Strategies for the Intermediate Grades*. Copyright © 2011 by Kendall Hunt Publishing Company (1-800-247-3458, ext. 4). May be reproduced for noncommercial educational purposes within the guidelines on the copyright page. www.kendallhunt.com/readingresources

Paired Questioning

Text Type	Narrative, Informational
When to Use	During Reading, After Reading
Comprehension Strategy	Monitoring Meaning, Using Prior Knowledge, Asking Questions, Inferring
How to Use	Partner

Description

Paired Questioning (McLaughlin & Allen, 2009; Vaughan & Estes, 1986) involves putting students in pairs, having them read short segments of narrative or informational text, and then questioning each other about its content. Paired Questioning is an adaptation of the ReQuest procedure developed by Manzo (1969). Paired Questioning gives students practice in developing questions on a variety of levels and helps students learn to select and defend their choices regarding the main ideas and important details in a text. _____

Teaching Goals Related to Learner Outcomes

1. To actively engage students in a reading selection.
2. To provide an opportunity for students to ask and answer questions while reading a selection.
3. To encourage students to ask a variety of questions.
4. To help students understand a reading selection.

Procedure

1. Divide the class into pairs of students.
2. Share the guidelines of the Paired Questioning procedure (see page 61) with students and explain it as needed.
3. After students understand the guidelines, have them read the title and/or chapter headings. Model the procedure by reading aloud to the class the title from the book, *Africa is Not a Country* (Knight & Melnicove, 2000). In this book, each page tells a short story about a child in a different country in Africa. Invite students to ask you questions about the book as in the following example.

   Teacher: I just read the title of the book aloud to you. Can one of you ask me a question about the book?

   Student: What countries do you think will be in the book?

   Teacher: I know the names of several countries in Africa, but instead of me telling you, why don't we brainstorm the ones we all know? [List all the African countries the class knows.]

   Teacher: I think we answered your question. Now I have a question for you. What do you think will be different in the lives of these children from your own life?

4. After a student has answered your question, continue modeling Paired Questioning with a page from the book as follows.

> Teacher: I'm going to read the page about the country of Kenya. After reading I'd like someone to ask me a question that I can answer from the passage.
>
> Student: How do students get to school?
>
> Teacher: They run to school. Now I'm going to ask a question. What do the children hope to be able to do in the future?
>
> Student: They hope to run marathons outside of Kenya.

5. Continue to model the Paired Questioning strategy until you believe the students understand how to proceed with a partner. Then refer students again to the Paired Questioning Guidelines from page 61 and have them continue reading and posing questions with their partners.

6. In order to continue modeling good questioning techniques, you may want to use the strategy when reading aloud to students in small and large group settings.

7. Encourage students to ask questions of themselves as they read independently.

References

Knight, M. B., & Melnicove, M. (2000). *Africa is not a country*. Minneapolis, MN: Millbrook Press.

Manzo, A. V. (1969). ReQuest procedure. *Journal of Reading, 13*, 123–126.

McLaughlin, M., & Allen, M. B. (2009). *Guided comprehension: A teaching model for grades 3–8* (2nd ed.). Newark, DE: International Reading Association.

Vaughan, J. L., & Estes, T. H. (1986). *Reading and reasoning beyond the primary grades*. Boston: Allyn and Bacon.

Paired Questioning Guidelines

Getting Started

1. Find a quiet place.

2. Be sure you can see the words and illustrations clearly.

3. Read the title or heading to yourself.

4. Close the book or turn it over.

5. Ask your partner a question and listen to the answer.

6. Have your partner ask you a question. Answer it.

7. Be sure you and your partner agree on the answers to the questions. Reread to see if you are correct.

Keep Going

1. Read some more of the book to yourself. Think of another question to ask your partner.

2. Close the book again (or turn it over). Ask your partner your question and then try to answer your partner's question.

When You Are Finished Reading

1. Think of the most important ideas from your reading.

2. Tell your partner your ideas. Does your partner agree with you? What are your partner's ideas?

3. If you have time, draw a picture of the most important ideas from your reading and write a short summary of your reading to share with the rest of the class.

Jerry Johns, Susan Lenski, & Roberta Berglund. *Essential Comprehension Strategies for the Intermediate Grades*. Copyright © 2011 by Kendall Hunt Publishing Company (1-800-247-3458, ext. 4). May be reproduced for noncommercial educational purposes within the guidelines on the copyright page. www.kendallhunt.com/readingresources

Personality Profiles

Text Type	Narrative, Informational
When to Use	Before Reading, During Reading, After Reading
Comprehension Strategy	Using Prior Knowledge, Inferring, Determining Importance, Synthesizing
How to Use	Small Group, Whole Group

Description

Students are asked to develop a Personality Profile of a character, historical figure, or present-day person by reading a quotation and writing down as many words as possible that could describe the person quoted. Students work in different groups to generate words. Following discussion and reading, students revisit their words and assess the validity of the words and their appropriateness as they revise their original profiles. Buehl (2009) shares a similar strategy with examples of quotations from Anne Frank and Chief Joseph.

Teaching Goals Related to Learner Outcomes

1. To engage students in making predictions and inferences based on their background knowledge and a limited amount of information.
2. To have students synthesize and evaluate information after reading.
3. To help students determine the importance and accuracy of their predictions.

Procedure

1. Select three or more quotations from a selection, story, or text that come from a specific character, a historical figure, a present-day person, or an animal that talks. Write each quotation on a separate note card or piece of paper. Below, for example, are three quotations from a selection about Lou Gehrig.

    "I'm benching myself . . . for the good of the team."

    "Fans, for the last two weeks you have been reading about a bad break I got. Yet today I consider myself the luckiest man on the face of the earth."

    "So I close in saying that I might have had a bad break, but I have an awful lot to live for. Thank you."

2. Using the example above, separate the class into three groups and give each group a quotation.
3. Tell the groups to read the quotations, think what they might reveal about the character, and then write down as many words as possible that could be used to describe the person quoted. A reproducible for this purpose can be found on page 65. Provide copies for each group or each student.
4. Give students several minutes to write their words. Then bring the groups together and have students share their lists with the entire class. You may want to write the words on the board or invite a volunteer from each group to do so.

5. After all the words have been shared, tell students that the same person or character spoke the quotations. Invite student reactions and then develop a personality profile for the person or character by asking students to synthesize the words listed. Encourage reflective thinking as the personality profile is developed. Work with students to write a personality profile.

6. Give students the selection, story, or text to read. As students read, they can evaluate their profile based on the information in the selection.

7. After students have read the selection, have them make changes to the original profile. Then engage students in a class discussion as they develop a revised profile.

8. To extend the lesson, students could be encouraged to make up an original quotation that would likely be a good fit with the revised personality profile.

9. To expand the list of words that students might be able to use as part of future profiles, refer to Examples of Character Traits on page 23.

Reference

Buehl, D. (2009). *Classroom strategies for interactive learning* (3rd ed.). Newark, DE: International Reading Association.

Personality Profiles

Directions:

Read your quotation and write down as many words as possible that could be used to describe the person, character, or animal. When you have your list of words, use some of them to write a profile of the personality. After reading or listening to more information, revise your profile as needed.

_____   _____   _____

_____   _____   _____

_____   _____   _____

_____   _____   _____

Our Group Personality Profile

_____

_____

_____

_____

_____

Revised Personality Profile

_____

_____

_____

_____

_____

Question-Answer Relationships (QARs)

Text Type	Narrative, Informational
When to Use	Before Reading, After Reading
Comprehension Strategy	Using Prior Knowledge, Asking Questions, Inferring, Determining Importance, Synthesizing
How to Use	Individual, Partner, Small Group, Whole Group

Description

Question-Answer Relationships (QARs), designed for students in the middle and upper grades, was developed by Raphael (1982, 1984, 1986). It is a strategy to help students identify the different sources of information for answering questions. It also gives students language to use in talking about the strategy (Raphael & Au, 2005). The National Reading Panel (2000) supports the answering of questions as one way to help strengthen comprehension. There are four kinds of questions in QARs. Two of the question types are subsumed in a category called In the Book: Right There (students find the answer within a single sentence) and Think and Search (students need to piece together information from one or more texts). The other category of questions is called In My Head which is further divided into Author and Me and On My Own. Author and Me questions ask students to consider the author's perspective and/or position along with their own experiences to formulate a response. On My Own questions invite students to make a personal connection or evaluation related to something they have experienced or are experiencing. Using graphics in this lesson greatly aids the teaching and understanding of QARs.

Teaching Goals Related to Learner Outcomes

1. To improve students' abilities to answer questions.
2. To help students understand and analyze the task demands of questions.
3. To strengthen students' comprehension, test-taking skills, and ability to apply higher-level thinking to text.

Procedure

QARs are best taught over several days and practiced on a regular basis. For this reason, four different lessons are presented. They should be adapted to meet the needs of your students.

Lesson 1

1. It is helpful to have charts or overhead transparencies showing the separate types of QARs as well as their relationships to each other. The graphics that follow are also available on pages 72–73. It is wise to limit the initial lesson to In the Book QARs. To introduce the concept of QARs, you might say the following.

> I want to help you learn about different kinds of questions and the best way to answer them. Take a look at the chart. [Students may also be given a copy of the chart.] QARs stands for Question-Answer Relationships. That means that there is a relationship or connection between a question and where to find the answer. Let's learn about the different kinds of QARs.

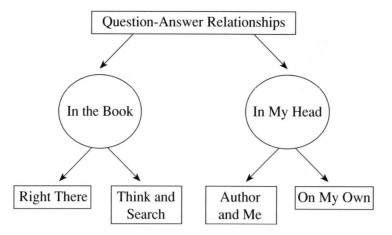

2. Focus on the first type of In the Book QAR. You might say the following.

> Look at the circle where it says In the Book. Under the circle are two types or kinds of questions that can be asked: Right There and Think and Search. The answer to a Right There question is right there in a book. It can be found in one place in a book or text.

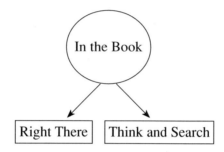

3. Show the Right There graphic or display it in chart form. Use an actual example from classroom materials to illustrate this type of QAR or a simple sentence like *The Nile is the longest river in the world*. Ask "What is the world's longest river?" and have students answer the question and point to where the answer can be found. Ask students to name this type of QAR. Then share some examples of phrases that are likely to suggest a Right There question:

Where is . . .?	When did . . .?	Who is . . .?
When is . . .?	What is . . .?	How many . . .?

4. Continue with the Think and Search QAR in a manner similar to that above. You could say the following.

> You can see that there is a second kind of QAR related to In the Book. What is it? [Think and Search]. To answer this type of question, you have to put together information from different parts of the book or text.

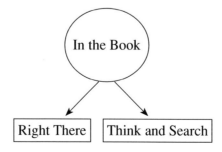

5. Show the Think and Search graphic or display it in chart form. Be sure students understand that the answer comes from different parts of the book. It may not be on the same page. The answer may also use different words than the message in the text. In addition, sometimes the answer may come from two

different texts. Provide an example to help illustrate this type of QAR. For example, *The Nile River is an important source of fresh water. Many people farm in the fertile Nile River Valley.* Ask "Why is the Nile important?" Have students answer the question. Be sure to note that the answer is not in one place and that students will need to do some thinking and searching. You may want to offer a few phrases that are likely to require students to Think and Search. Several examples follow:

Why was . . .?	How did . . .?
What reasons . . .?	What caused . . .?

6. Use other examples from classroom materials where students must search more than a single page to find the answer. Have students identify this type of QAR.

7. Create opportunities for students to practice what you have taught. Use passages composed of two or three sentences. You can create the passages or find them in classroom materials. Develop questions for the passages. Give the passages and questions to students along with identifying the QAR in words. Discuss the answers and make connections to the passages. Below are examples.

The Ganges River is in southern Asia. It is a holy river for Hindus.

 What is special about the Ganges?

It is a holy river.

A rain forest is a warm, wet area. Tall trees and vines grow there. Many other types of plants can be found in the rain forest.

 What grows in a rain forest?

tall trees, vines, and many types of plants

8. Provide a second opportunity for students to practice. Give students passages, questions, and correct answers to the questions. Students, as a group, should identify the type of QAR for each question. Clarify student responses as needed.

9. A final stage of practice involves passages and questions. Students should read the passages, determine the QARs, and write the answers. Ample time should be spent in having students think aloud to explain their reasoning.

Lesson 2

1. Review the first lesson. Then teach the two types of In My Head QARs. Use a procedure similar to Lesson 1. In addition, provide practice opportunities that extend the learning to include all four types of QARs. Be sure to use examples and materials that are of interest to your students. The remaining part of this lesson will highlight the general procedure. Refer to ideas from Lesson 1 as needed and transfer them to this lesson.

2. Tell students that they will be learning about more QARs. Present the chart in the classroom and say the following.

You have been learning about the two kinds of QARs that are In the Book. [Review them briefly.] Today we will learn about the QARs that are In My Head. Who can tell me one of them? [Invite a student to respond.] That's right. It's called Author and Me. You know that the author is the person who writes the material or book. Sometimes you are asked to use information from the author along with information already in your head to make an answer. What you already know in your head can be used to help you answer the question. [Make sure that students know that their background knowledge is a relevant source in answering these types of questions. Use an example from your classroom materials and model the process for students.]

3. Share some examples of phrases that may be used for Author and Me questions:

Do you agree with . . .?	Would you . . .?
In your view, which character . . .?	What else . . .?
What did you think of . . .?	Why might . . .?

4. Continue with a description of the On My Own type of question. You could say the following.

> Now let's look at the last kind of QAR. It's called On My Own. The answer is not in the text. You need to use your own ideas and experiences to answer the question. Before reading, I could ask what you already know about a certain topic. Your answer would come from your previous knowledge and experience. Suppose we read a story about a person who is very excited. I could ask, "What do you do when you are excited?" You could answer even though you have not read the story. [Provide additional examples so students can express feelings and understandings.]

5. Share some examples of phrases that may signal On My Own questions:

Do you know . . .?	Would you like . . .?
Would you ever . . .?	What would you . . .?

6. Create or use materials to provide practice along the lines of Lesson 1. Proceed in a systematic and intentional manner in order to help solidify and extend student learning.

Lesson 3

1. The focus of this lesson is to provide passages of 75–150 words so students can practice QARs in a natural reading situation.

2. Review each QAR category using the QAR chart. Then present the passage and five questions that use the various QARs. It is useful to do the first passage as a group and provide feedback and guidance as necessary.

3. Provide a second passage and questions that students complete independently. Engage students in discussion to justify their answers and the QAR identified. If necessary, explain why a particular answer is acceptable. In some cases, students may be able to justify more than one answer.

4. Use a similar procedure with subsequent passages.

Lesson 4 and Beyond

1. Tell students that these lessons are practice opportunities using passages that approximate the length of students' typical reading.

2. Select a passage approximately the length of a short story. Divide the passage into four sections and create two questions for each QAR with the exception of On My Own. Have students identify the QAR type and answer the question.

3. Use the first section as a way to review and reinforce the strategy. Students should complete the remaining three sections independently.

4. Have students share their responses to each of the three sections. Provide rich opportunities for discussion and interaction. Provide appropriate feedback as needed.

5. Subsequent lessons should provide opportunities to use QARs with both narrative and informational passages read in their entirety. Depending on the length of the passage, create up to six questions for Right There, Think and Search, and Author and Me (a total of 18 questions). Students should read the passage independently, determine the QAR for each question, and answer the questions. Class discussion, appropriate feedback, and guidance should be provided. Spend ample time discussing the

questions and the kind of thinking involved in answering them. It can help students realize different levels of thinking and the role of text, background knowledge, and experience. Students should gain greater awareness of their thinking processes or metacognition.

Additional Tips for Using QARs
Raphael, 1986

1. Too many Right There QARs may indicate an overemphasis on literal, detail questions.

2. Think and Search QARs should dominate because they require integration of information and should build to asking Author and Me QARs.

3. On My Own QARs are designed to help students think about what they already know and how it relates to an upcoming story or content text. They can also be used after reading to help students react. For example, Would you like to be a biologist?

4. For extension activities, create primarily On My Own or Author and Me QARs to activate students' background information as it pertains to the text.

5. QARs initially help students understand that information from both texts and their background knowledge is important to consider when answering questions.

6. QARs can help students determine text structures in informational text (compare/contrast, cause/effect, list/example, explanation).

7. QARs help students realize that some information for a question may not be in the text, and it is necessary to read between or beyond the lines to draw appropriate conclusions and inferences.

References

National Reading Panel. (2000). *Teaching children to read: An evidence-based assessment of the scientific research literature on reading and its implications for reading instruction.* Washington, DC: National Institute for Child Health & Human Development.

Raphael, T. E. (1982). Question-answering strategies for children. *The Reading Teacher, 36,* 186–190.

Raphael, T. E. (1984). Teaching learners about sources of information for answering comprehension questions. *Journal of Reading, 27,* 303–311.

Raphael, T. E. (1986). Teaching question-answer relationships, revisited. *The Reading Teacher, 39,* 516–522.

Raphael, T. E. & Au, K. H. (2005). QAR: Enhancing comprehension and test taking across grades and content areas. *The Reading Teacher, 59,* 206–221.

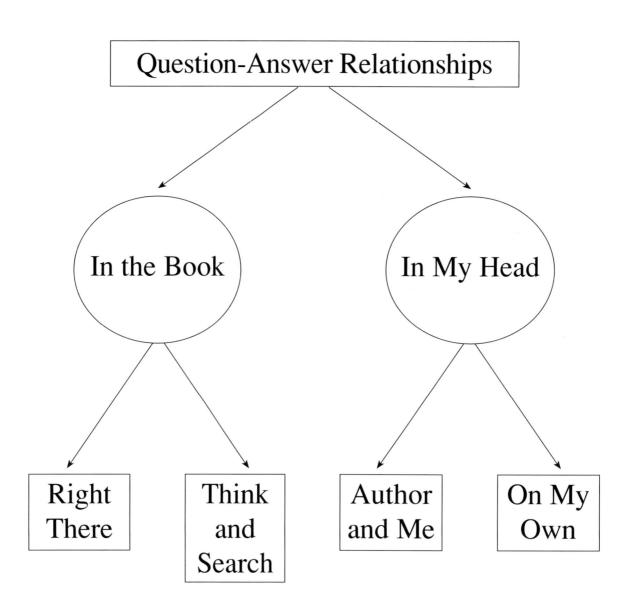

Question-Answer Relationships

In the Book

In My Head

Right There

Think and Search

Author and Me

On My Own

Question-Answer Relationships (QARs)

In the Book	**In My Head**
Right There  It's right there! The answer to this question can be found in one place in the text.	On My Own   This type of question invites you to make a personal connection to something you have experienced or are experiencing.
Think and Search  To arrive at the answer to this question you need to piece together different parts of one or more texts.	Author and Me  The response to this question asks you to consider the author's perspective/position and your own experiences and views to formulate a response.

Question-Answer Relationships (QARs)

Question: _____

Answer: _____
_____

☐ Right There
☐ Think and Search
☐ Author and Me
☐ On My Own

Question: _____

Answer: _____
_____

☐ Right There
☐ Think and Search
☐ Author and Me
☐ On My Own

Question: _____

Answer: _____
_____

☐ Right There
☐ Think and Search
☐ Author and Me
☐ On My Own

Reciprocal Teaching

Text Type	Narrative, Informational
When to Use	Before Reading, During Reading, After Reading
Comprehension Strategy	Monitoring Meaning, Using Prior Knowledge, Asking Questions, Inferring, Synthesizing
How to Use	Individual, Partner, Small Group, Whole Group

Description

Reciprocal Teaching was developed by Brown and Palincsar (1984) as a way to improve reading comprehension through active thinking. Reciprocal Teaching helps students refine four different comprehension strategies: questioning, clarifying, summarizing, and predicting.

Teaching Goals Related to Learner Outcomes

1. To encourage students to use questioning, clarifying, summarizing, and predicting as they read.
2. To provide students with practice on asking and answering questions about text.
3. To help students improve their comprehension by incorporating more than one strategy at a time.

Procedure

1. Select an unfamiliar narrative or informational book or passage for students to read such as *The Salmon Princess* (Dwyer, 2004). This story is the Alaskan version of Cinderella and, although most students will know at least one version of Cinderella, they will probably not know this one.
2. Duplicate and distribute copies of the Reciprocal Teaching (Oczkus, 2010) reproducible on page 78. Show students the cover of the book and read the title. Ask students to make predictions about the book based on this information. An example follows.

Predicting	Questioning	Clarifying	Summarizing
The story will be set in Alaska.			
They have lots of salmon in Alaska.			
There are lots of rivers.			

3. Read the first several pages of *The Salmon Princess* aloud to students or have them read it in groups. Ask students to develop questions about the book that will promote their comprehension. For example, you could say something like the following.

> When good readers read a new book, they make predictions about what they will be reading. We've already made some predictions. As you read, you should also ask questions about your reading that you hope will be answered. The questions should stem from the predictions you've made, but they might also come from new information. Here are a few questions I asked as I began reading the book. I'll write them on the Reciprocal Teaching reproducible.

Predicting	Questioning	Clarifying	Summarizing
	Where is SE Alaska and how close is it to Canada?		
	Is this a rain forest?		
	What did they do with the salmon?		

4. Ask the students to generate their own questions. Write the questions that students generate on the Reciprocal Teaching reproducible after yours. Then divide the class into small groups. Have students select one or more questions to discuss in their groups.

5. After students have discussed the questions, explain that sometimes they will find the answers to their questions in their reading and sometimes they won't.

6. Then tell students that there may be sections in the text that are unclear and that need to be clarified. Tell students that good readers monitor or keep track of their comprehension by looking for parts that are not clear. Have students discuss areas that need to be clarified in their groups. If students need parts of the story clarified, write those parts on the Reciprocal Teaching reproducible as follows.

Predicting	Questioning	Clarifying	Summarizing
		SE Alaska is a rain forest with lots of rain, water falls, and rivers.	
		Salmon is a big part of their culture.	
		Many people fish.	

7. Remind students that summarizing helps them remember what they have read. Tell students that they can summarize during reading as well as after reading. Have students summarize what they know from their reading thus far. An example follows.

Predicting	Questioning	Clarifying	Summarizing
			The people in SE Alaska live in a very rainy area with lots of rivers.
			Their culture is about fishing and salmon.
			The princess is like Cinderella, but she lived differently from the other Cinderella stories I've heard.

8. Have students practice the strategies of predicting, questioning, clarifying, and summarizing in small groups during reading. As students become adept at these strategies, have one member of the group act as the leader and guide the discussion. Rotate leaders so that each student has the opportunity of being a group member and a leader.

9. Encourage students to use the strategies of predicting, questioning, clarifying, and summarizing independently as they read.

References

Brown, A. L., & Palincsar, A. S. (1984). Reciprocal teaching of comprehension: Fostering and monitoring activities. *Cognition and Instruction, 1*, 117–175.

Dwyer, M. (2004). *The salmon princess: An Alaskan Cinderella story.* Seattle, WA: Sasquatch Books.

Oczkus, L. D. (2010). *Reciprocal teaching at work: Powerful strategies and lessons for improving reading comprehension* (2nd ed.). Newark, DE: International Reading Association.

Reciprocal Teaching

Predicting	Questioning	Clarifying	Summarizing

Semantic Mapping

Text Type	Narrative, Informational
When to Use	Before Reading, During Reading, After Reading
Comprehension Strategy	Determining Importance, Synthesizing
How to Use	Individual, Small Group

Description

Semantic Mapping (Heimlich & Pittelman, 1986; Johnson & Pearson, 1984; Pearson & Johnson, 1978) helps students bridge what they know about a topic and what they learn from information in the text or from another information source. Semantic Mapping actively involves students in graphically organizing information in categorical form. The four-step strategy (brainstorming, categorizing, reading, and revising the categories) helps students to become active readers and, in the process, remember new vocabulary and information.

Teaching Goals Related to Learner Outcomes

1. To help students activate and organize knowledge about a specific topic.
2. To help students graphically see relationships among words.
3. To have students classify words into superordinate and subordinate concepts.
4. To help students expand their vocabularies.

Procedure

1. Choose a major concept or topic being studied by the class. In elementary science, for example, sea life is one topic students learn about. The seahorse is one kind of sea life that students find especially fascinating.

2. Draw an oval on the board. You can also use the reproducible on page 81. Write *seahorses* in the center of the oval. Ask students to brainstorm words related to their study of *seahorses*. For example, words might be *tails, fins, pouch, fish, snout, bony plates, crabs, change color, thousand babies*. List words related to the topic on the board.

3. When the brainstormed words have been listed, read them aloud and ask students to think of headings that the words might be clustered under. Students need to label their clusters or give them titles to indicate what the words have in common. Put cluster headings in the ovals surrounding the center oval. You may wish to have students complete this step in small cooperative groups. It is often possible for some of the brainstormed words to become category headings. For example, the labels for clusters related to the seahorse might be *How They Look, How They Reproduce, What They Eat*, and *How They Survive*.

4. Next, have students try to put the brainstormed words on lines branching from the appropriate oval, showing connections to the idea within the oval. When you and the students have completed the classification and categorization of the words, invite students to share the labels for each of their clusters and the words they have included under each heading. You may wish to record these on the board.

5. It is important that students share their reasons for their clustering decisions. This sharing stimulates students to think of the words in a variety of ways, consider their meanings, connect them, and see relationships among the words.

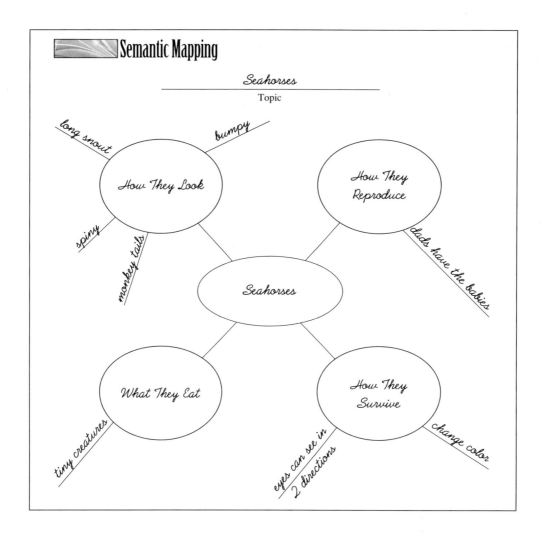

Semantic Mapping

Seahorses
Topic

- long snout
- bumpy
- spiny
- monkey tails

How They Look

How They Reproduce

- dads have the babies

Seahorses

What They Eat

How They Survive

- tiny creatures
- eyes can see in 2 directions
- change color

6. If used as a prereading activity, ask students to then read the text and evaluate their headings and the words they have clustered together. They may need to rename some of their headings and/or rearrange some words based on additional information in the lesson.

7. If used as a postreading activity, students may want to return to the text and confirm their accuracy and reasons for their clusters and connected words.

8. The strategy work can be extended over the course of several days as students acquire additional information about the topic. More words can be added to the clusters as students expand their knowledge and increase the connections they make between and among the words. If desired, different colored inks can be used for words added from additional sources or at different times, thus graphically illustrating the expanding knowledge base of the students and the desirability of using a variety of resources in acquiring information.

9. When the semantic maps are complete, have students work individually or in pairs to write a summary of the information in one of the clusters or write a longer piece about the topic, using each one of the clusters of information as a paragraph in a main idea-detail piece. Students may also use their completed semantic maps as study aids.

References

Heimlich, J. E., & Pittelman, S. D. (1986). *Semantic mapping: Classroom applications.* Newark, DE: International Reading Association.

Johnson, D. D., & Pearson, P. D. (1984). *Teaching reading vocabulary* (2nd ed.). New York: Holt, Rinehart & Winston.

Pearson, P. D., & Johnson, D. D. (1978). *Teaching reading comprehension.* New York: Holt, Rinehart & Winston.

Name _____ Date _____

Semantic Mapping

_____
Topic

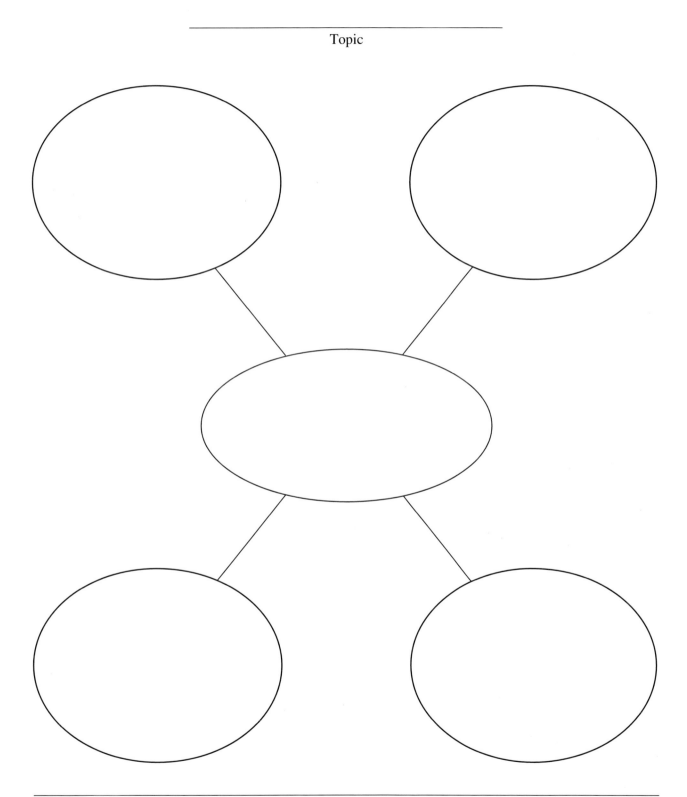

Name _____   Date _____

Semantic Mapping

Topic _____

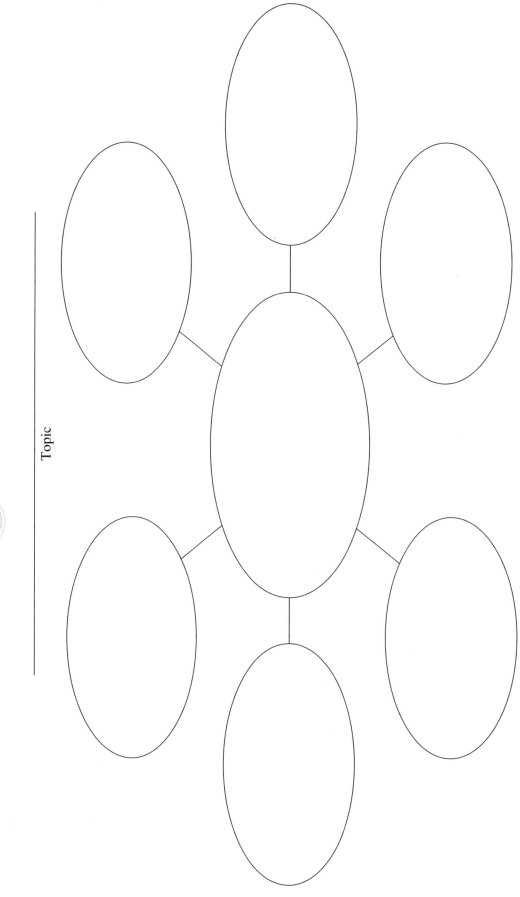

Sketch to Stretch

Text Type	Narrative, Informational
When to Use	After Reading
Comprehension Strategy	Inferring, Creating Images, Synthesizing
How to Use	Partner, Small Group, Whole Group

Description

Sketch to Stretch (Short, Harste, & Burke, 1996) is a strategy that offers students a way to extend meaning and respond to narrative text, informational text, or poetry following reading. Sketch to Stretch assists students in using visualization to support comprehension (McLaughlin & Allen, 2009). It also can be used as a means to help students become more comfortable in talking and working in pairs and in small groups. After students read or listen to a selection, they are asked to draw a sketch showing what the passage means to them. Sketch to Stretch can be introduced and modeled during class read-aloud experiences and can then be moved into small group settings to encourage rich discussions.

Teaching Goals Related to Learner Outcomes

1. To extend the opportunities for students to respond after reading a selection.
2. To help students visualize emotions they feel during reading.
3. To provide students with opportunities to extend meanings from texts.

Procedure

1. Read a selected text aloud to students and model a think-aloud while doing so. For example, while reading the real-life story, *The Librarian of Basra* (Winter, 2005), you might say something like the following.

   > As I look at the cover of this book, I see a woman dressed with a headscarf surrounded by books. The title of the book lets me know that the woman is a librarian and that she lives in Iraq. I wonder what will happen to the woman in this story.

   > [Read the book to students. Pause during the story and have students predict what they think will happen.]

   > This librarian was really brave. She hid the library books when the war came to her city. I wonder if she was afraid when the library was bombed. I know I would be. I also wonder if the books are still safe. I know that the American Library Association has a fund to rebuild the library. I hope the people of Basra can still use the books. I know I use my local library all of the time.

2. After finishing the read-aloud and think-aloud, introduce the idea of making a drawing of the feelings students have about the text. Say something like the following.

   > I'm going to try to sketch what I was thinking as I read. When I finish, I want you to guess what you think I was remembering and thinking about. I am not going to color my picture or make it ready to hang on the bulletin board in the classroom. I am just going to keep my sketch in my journal so I can remember something about this book, how I felt while I read it, and a connection I made while

reading. [Draw a picture of a woman, books, and hearts to represent how much the librarian loved books.]

3. Have students hypothesize about your interpretation of the book and explain by saying something like the following.

   I drew a sketch of a woman wearing a headscarf, a pile of books, and hearts all around it. That's because I thought about how much the librarian must have loved the books to risk hiding them. I really love books too, and I can't imagine what it would be like for a city to have all of their books destroyed. It also reminded me of a local school that had a fire last year. They weren't able to save their library, but other schools donated enough books to replace them. I hope they can rebuild the library in Basra.

4. Give students an opportunity to draw sketches of their ideas about the book on the Sketch to Stretch reproducible from page 85.

5. After students have drawn their sketches, ask them to write what the sketch was about, how they felt about the sketch, and the connections they made.

6. When students have finished their sketches, invite each student to show his or her sketch. Before each student shares the sketch, consider asking the other students to hypothesize what the sketch is about. This is effective in some classes but not in others, so be sensitive to how the class responds.

7. Continue sharing sketches until most students have shared or until students understand the procedures for Sketch to Stretch.

8. Explain to students that they will be using Sketch to Stretch in their small groups or partner time and that they can use this strategy independently to visualize ideas while reading.

References

McLaughlin, M., & Allen, M. B. (2009). *Guided comprehension: A teaching model for grades 3–8* (2nd ed.). Newark, DE: International Reading Association.

Short, K. G., Harste, J. C., & Burke, C. (1996). *Creating classrooms for authors and inquirers* (2nd ed.). Portsmouth, NH: Heinemann.

Winter, J. (2005). *The librarian of Basra*. New York: Harcourt.

Sketch to Stretch

_____
Title

This sketch is about _____

_____

_____

I feel _____

_____

_____

I made a connection to _____

_____

_____

Stop, Predict, Support (SPS)

Text Type	Narrative, Informational
When to Use	Before Reading, During Reading, After Reading
Comprehension Strategy	Using Prior Knowledge, Asking Questions, Inferring, Creating Images, Synthesizing
How to Use	Individual, Partner, Small Group, Whole Group

Description

The Stop, Predict, Support (SPS) strategy encourages students to use text to support the predictions they make during reading. When some students read, they sometimes make predictions from their imaginations that are not text-based. The SPS strategy invites students to use their text to make predictions rather than making predictions from their imaginations alone.

Teaching Goals Related to Learner Outcomes

1. To encourage students to make predictions while reading.
2. To invite students to identify text that supports their predictions.
3. To encourage students to reflect on the predictions that they make.
4. To help students understand how knowledge of text structure assists comprehension.

Procedure

1. To introduce this strategy, identify a book or book chapter that you can read with students that has an element of the unknown. (Most students find that making predictions is easier with narrative texts. Once they are comfortable with the strategy, you can use it with informational texts.) Read the book before the lesson and select three places to stop and make predictions.

2. Write the title of the book on the top of the Stop, Predict, Support (SPS) reproducible as in the example of *The Three Little Hawaiian Pigs and the Magic Shark* (Laird, 1981) that follows. Some students will know another version of the story which will help them make general predictions. For the SPS strategy, however, students will need to pay close attention to make predictions for this particular text.

3. Read the title of the selection to students showing them the cover of the book. Model ways to use information about the title and cover as support for predictions. Ask students to make predictions about the contents of the book by using the words in the title as in the following example.

   Teacher: The title of the book is *The Three Little Hawaiian Pigs and the Magic Shark*. It is the Hawaiian version of a story you might know. You can see the picture on the front cover. What do you notice about the title and cover?

   Student: I see a shark dressed up and selling "shave ice."

   Teacher: Do you think this will be a true story about sharks? What do you think will happen?

   Student: No, this shark is not pictured in the water.

   Teacher: Good, you based your prediction on the illustration. Let's see what happens in the book.

4. Distribute blank copies of the SPS reproducible on page 90 to students. Write the words *prediction* and *support* on the board. Tell students that they will be making predictions about the story and that their predictions must have support. Review with students what it means to make predictions about stories. Then tell students that support means to tell *why* they made predictions. Emphasize that their reasons for predictions must be based on the content or illustrations from the story. To explain support, you might say something like the following:

> I know many of you make predictions when you read. In class discussions, I've asked you why you made your predictions. Today, though, I'd like you to make your predictions based on evidence from the story. You will use it to support your predictions.

5. Read up to the first stopping place in the story you have selected for this lesson. After reading, point out the STOP sign on the SPS chart. Tell students that the STOP sign is there to remind them to stop while reading and make predictions.

6. Demonstrate how to make predictions using text as a support. Show students an example of a prediction and text support as in the example based on the story as follows. Read the first prediction.

> Prediction: The first pig will make a grass house.

> Support: The pigs left home and saw the man with a load of pili grass on the way. The first pig wanted to go fishing—not spend time building a house.

7. Read the next section of the story and continue modeling making predictions with the support of the text. Use the sample on page 89 to demonstrate this strategy.

8. After you have modeled SPS with predictions and support that you have provided, ask students if they understand what it means to support their predictions with text. Work collaboratively with the students to make predictions and support them using the SPS strategy.

9. Once students understand the process of SPS, have them make predictions and support using the SPS strategy with you. Select a book for students to stop and make predictions. Ask students to write their predictions on the SPS reproducible. Then have students identify the text segment that supports their predictions and write that support next to their predictions. Provide assistance as needed.

10. Provide guidance until students are able to use the SPS strategy to make predictions with text support independently. You can use the SPS strategy with narrative and informational texts. Once students are able to support their predictions, give them the SPS reproducible found on page 90 to use during independent reading.

11. Remind students that the SPS strategy is one that they should use whenever they read. Tell students that they should make predictions using the text to support the predictions whenever they read at home or at school.

Reference

Laird, D. M. (1981). *The three little Hawaiian pigs and the magic shark*. Honolulu, HI: Barnaby Books.

The Three Little Hawaiian Pigs and the Magic Shark
Title

Prediction	Support
STOP The first pig will build a house with grass. p. _____	A man with pili grass went by.
STOP The magic shark will want to eat the pigs. p. _____	The shark saw the pigs out surfing. He then disguised himself as a "shave ice" man and knocked on their door.
STOP The lei seller is the magic shark. p. _____	The shark can turn himself into other forms. He was still trying to eat the pigs by coming to their house in disguise.

Name _____ Date _____

Title _____

Stop, Predict, Support

Prediction	Support
STOP p. _____	
STOP p. _____	
STOP p. _____	

Story Board

Text Type	Narrative
When to Use	After Reading
Comprehension Strategy	Using Prior Knowledge, Inferring, Creating Images, Synthesizing
How to Use	Individual, Partner, Small Group, Whole Group

Description

A Story Board is a series of frames that can be used to outline a narrative text. Story Boards can show events in a series and can be written and/or illustrated. Students read or listen to a story and determine the beginning, middle, and end or the events that take place in the plot. Story Boards can help students learn how texts are organized.

Teaching Goals Related to Learner Outcomes

1. To help students understand that narrative texts have a beginning, middle, and end.
2. To help students identify the events that take place in the plot of a narrative story.

Procedure

1. Identify a story that has a clear beginning, middle, and end or that has events in a series that can be easily discerned. An example of such a story is *Listen to the Wind* (Mortenson & Roth, 2009). This story is about a man, Dr. Greg, who builds schools in Pakistan.

2. Teach students about the organization of narrative texts. Younger students should learn that narratives have a beginning, middle, and end. Students who understand those basic concepts can learn that stories have events that take place in order.

3. Read the story or have students read the story in groups. As students are listening to the story, have them think about the events that occurred.

4. Provide students with a blank copy of the Story Board from page 93. One group of three frames is sufficient for students who are drawing a beginning, middle, and end.

5. Guide students to think about the sections of the story as in the example that follows.

    Teacher: This story is set in Korphe, Pakistan and the main character is Greg Mortenson, an American. What happens at the beginning of the story?

    Student 1: Dr. Greg stumbles into the village.

    Teacher: What was he doing in Pakistan?

    Student 2: He was climbing a mountain.

    Teacher: Let's put that all into a sentence so we can remember what happened in the beginning of the story. [Create sentences with students.] Now let's think about what happened in the middle of the story.

    Student 3: The people in the village helped Dr. Greg by giving him food.

Student 4: Dr. Greg wanted to help the village for saving his life.

Student 5: Dr. Greg learned that they wanted a school in the village.

Teacher: Yes, all of these things happened in the middle of the story. What kind of picture would you draw to represent the middle of the story? [Elicit student responses.] I'm going to draw a picture of Dr. Greg talking with the men of Korphe. Now what happened at the end?

Student: Dr. Greg came back to build a school, but he had to build a bridge first.

Teacher: Yes, he was able to get money to build a school in Korphe. That's the ending of the story and would fit in the last section of the Story Board.

6. Have students draw a picture of the beginning of the story. Older students can write a sentence under each illustration. Make sure students understand the directions before continuing.

7. Guide students in determining the middle and end of the story. Ask them to illustrate these parts of the story and to label or write sentences about them. Older students can write several events that occurred in the story. Make sure students write them in the order they occurred in the book.

8. Have students share their Story Boards with others in the class.

9. Remind students that narrative texts have a beginning, middle, and end and include a series of events.

Reference

Mortenson, G., & Roth, S. L. (2009). *Listen to the wind: The story of Dr. Greg and three cups of tea*. New York: Dial Books.

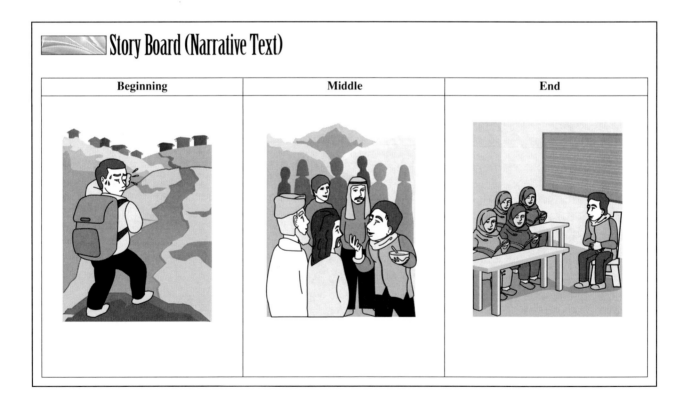

Story Board (Narrative Text)

Beginning	Middle	End

Name _____ Date _____

Title _____

Story Board

Beginning	Middle	End

Story Maps

Text Type	Narrative
When to Use	After Reading
Comprehension Strategy	Using Prior Knowledge, Inferring, Creating Images, Synthesizing
How to Use	Individual, Small Group, Whole Group

Description

Understanding the elements of narrative text structure is an essential part of comprehending stories. One way for students to visualize how stories are organized is through Story Mapping. Story Maps are typically graphic organizers that have a place for the elements of narrative texts: setting, characters, events, problem, and solution. There are many ways that stories can be mapped.

Teaching Goals Related to Learner Outcomes

1. To help students identify the elements of narrative text to assist comprehension.
2. To help students visualize story elements by representing story elements in a graphic organizer.
3. To provide students with a way to think about how story elements relate to each other.

Procedure

1. Select a picture book that has clearly identified story elements. For example, the books in the Curious George series usually have a limited number of main characters, a clear problem, and events that lead to a resolution of the problem.
2. Make a display of the blank Story Map on page 98 or use the completed version on page 97 and duplicate copies for students.
3. Write the words *setting, characters, problem, events*, and *solution* on an overhead transparency or on the board. Review the words with students and remind them of the meaning of the words. You could say something like what follows.

   Today when I read to you, I would like you to think about the main parts of the story as you listen. Let's review the things that all stories have in common. First, there is a setting. The setting is where and when the story takes place. Stories also have characters. Characters can be animals or people. The characters are who the story is about. Stories also have a problem. The problem leads the characters to take some actions to solve it. What happens are the events of the story. The event that solves the problem is called the solution. Now that we have reviewed the main elements of a story, let's read!

4. Read the story, *Curious George Rides a Bike* (Rey, 1952) to the students.
5. After reading the story to the group, complete a Story Map together as follows.

   Most of you are familiar with Curious George stories from your younger years. In this story, George receives a bicycle from his owner, the man with the yellow hat. We are going to take a look at this story and identify the story elements so we can place them on a story map.

Please write the title of the book in the first space. Now think of the setting and write that in the next space. The setting will be the time and place of the story. What are the time and place that the story takes place? [present time, any place]

There is one main character in the book and several minor characters. List the main character in the next line and select one of the minor characters to write as well. [Curious George, man with the yellow hat, newspaper boy]

Next we need to consider the problem of the story. All stories have a problem, or something that the main character is trying to do or achieve. [Accept all reasonable answers.]

Narrative texts are developed using events in a series. Most of the stories you read will have the events in chronological order. List the events that happened in the story. [Accept all reasonable answers.]

Finally, I'd like you to think about how the problem was solved. In this book, George has lots of adventures, but he also learns how to ride his bike safely and responsibly. Write what you think is the solution to the problem in the next space.

After reading a story, you should also picture or retell it in your mind. Think about this story and write a summary in one or two sentences.

6. To conclude the lesson, review the story elements one more time and remind students to think about the things all stories have in common. Remind them that knowing these elements will help them better understand stories when they are reading.

7. Use each of the Story Maps on pages 98–99 throughout the year to provide students with several methods of representing story elements.

Reference

Rey, H. A. (1952). *Curious George rides a bike*. New York: Houghton Mifflin.

Story Map

Title	Curious George Rides a Bike

Setting	Present time, Anywhere

Characters	Curious George, man with yellow hat

Problem	Behaving responsibly with a gift.

Events

Curious George gets a bicycle as a gift.

↓

George helps a friend deliver newspapers.

↓

Bike is ruined, but George rides anyway.

↓

George rides bicycle in animal show.

↓

George is rescued by his owner.

Solution/Outcome	George learns how to ride a bike safely.

What is this story really about?

Curious George is given a bicycle but predictably gets into trouble.

George learns how to ride his bike safely and act responsibly.

Name _____ Date _____

 Story Map

Title

Setting

Characters

Problem

Events

↓

↓

↓

↓

Solution/Outcome

What is this story really about?

_____

_____

_____

_____

Jerry Johns, Susan Lenski, & Roberta Berglund. *Essential Comprehension Strategies for the Intermediate Grades*. Copyright © 2011 by Kendall Hunt Publishing Company (1-800-247-3458, ext. 4). May be reproduced for noncommercial educational purposes within the guidelines on the copyright page. www.kendallhunt.com/readingresources

Story Map

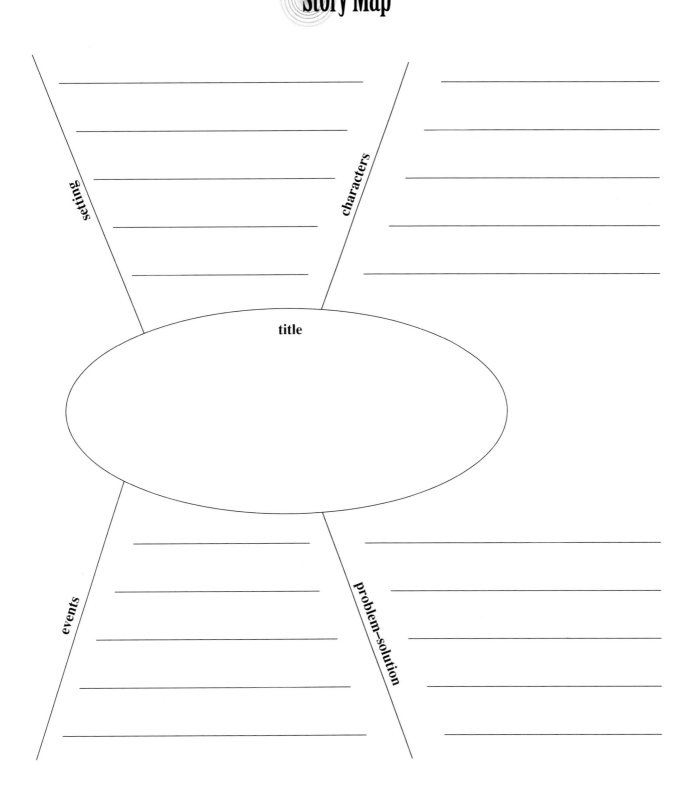

setting

characters

title

events

problem–solution

Text Coding

Text Type	Narrative, Informational
When to Use	During Reading
Comprehension Strategy	Monitoring Meaning, Using Prior Knowledge, Asking Questions, Inferring, Creating Images, Determining Importance, Synthesizing
How to Use	Individual, Partner, Small Group

Description

Text Coding (Harvey & Goudvis, 2007; Tovani, 2000; Vaughn & Estes, 1986) is a strategy to help students track their thinking as they read. Using a simple coding system, students make notations in the margins of the text or on sticky notes. Text Coding encourages students to monitor their comprehension as they read. It also enhances long-term retention of what was read. Text codes can increase in number and complexity depending on students' maturity, comfort, and experience in using them.

Teaching Goals Related to Learner Outcomes

1. To help students monitor their comprehension as they read.
2. To encourage students to respond to their reading and interact with the text.
3. To enable students to retain more information from reading.

Procedure

You will need:

2 sticky notes cut into 4 strips, each with the adhesive on one end
or 8 page markers, each with adhesive on one end
(You may wish to use different colored markers, one for each text code)

1. Select a text at the students' instructional level. In appropriate texts, students will recognize at least 95% of the words and have satisfactory (75%) comprehension.
2. Tell students how readers talk with themselves as they are reading: asking questions, agreeing or disagreeing with the author, and so on.
3. Read a portion of the selected text aloud to your students and model your thinking as you read. For example, when reading about seahorses (Kranking, 2010), and the text states that they change color to

match their surroundings, you might say, "I already knew that!" and place a sticky note with a √ on the sentence. When reading that seahorses' eyes can look in opposite directions, you might exclaim, "Wow, that's amazing, I didn't know that!" and add a sticky note with an exclamation mark on that portion of the text. You might also say, "I wonder about that," or "This doesn't make sense to me," if portions of the text are confusing. To introduce Text Coding, you may wish to limit the number of response possibilities until students become familiar with them and have several opportunities to use them. You may wish to duplicate copies of Our Text Codes on page 103 and distribute them for student use as they are learning the codes. Later, you might add additional response options from the Suggested Text Codes below.

Suggested Text Codes

Code Symbol	Meaning
*	Very important information; key concept; new information
?	Confusing information; something doesn't make sense; question
!	Wow! Something you find interesting, hard to believe, or unexpected
√	Something you already knew
V	Something you can visualize, make a picture in your mind
P	You can make a prediction
2+2	You put ideas together (synthesize)
X	Something you disagree with or that contradicts what you thought
R	Reminds you of something
T-S	Text-to-Self connection
T-T	Text-to-Text connection
T-W	Text-to-World connection

4. Each time you comment, show how you mark the text, either by marginal notation or using a sticky note.

5. Select another portion of the text and continue marking your text while the students read silently.

6. Allow students an opportunity to share their thinking.

7. As students become more comfortable with the coding system, encourage them to read portions of the text silently, coding as they read, and then share their thinking with a partner.

8. At the conclusion of each section, invite students to share selective responses, such as their "Wows!" or "New Information." Students are often amazed that others have had similar responses to their own. These comments often lead to extended discussion of the text and to clarifications of confusing or misunderstood concepts.

References

Harvey, S., & Goudvis, A. (2007). *Strategies that work: Teaching comprehension for understanding and engagement* (2nd ed.). Portland, ME: Stenhouse.

Kranking, K. (2010). Seahorses. *Ranger Rick, 44*(3), 6–11.

Tovani, C. (2000). *I read it, but I don't get it: Comprehension strategies for adolescent readers.* Portland, ME: Stenhouse.

Vaughn, J. L., & Estes, T. H. (1986). *Reading and reasoning beyond the primary grades.* Boston: Allyn & Bacon.

Our Text Codes

Coding Key

*   Very important information, key concept, or new information

?   Confusing information; something doesn't make sense; question

!   Wow! Something you find interesting, hard to believe, or unexpected

√   Something you already knew

As you read,

○   Use your sticky notes or markers to note sections of the text that you find to be new, key, or important information (*), information that you are confused about or that doesn't make sense (?), information you find interesting, hard to believe or unexpected (!), or something you already knew (√).

○   As you place a marker, write the appropriate symbol on it.

○   You may need to move your markers as you read.

○   Be ready to discuss your ideas with a partner or the class.

- -

Our Text Codes

Coding Key

*   Very important information, key concept, or new information

?   Confusing information; something doesn't make sense; question

!   Wow! Something you find interesting, hard to believe, or unexpected

√   Something you already knew

As you read,

○   Use your sticky notes or markers to note sections of the text that you find to be new, key, or important information (*), information that you are confused about or that doesn't make sense (?), information you find interesting, hard to believe or unexpected (!), or something you already knew (√).

○   As you place a marker, write the appropriate symbol on it.

○   You may need to move your markers as you read.

○   Be ready to discuss your ideas with a partner or the class.

Venn Diagram

Text Type	Narrative, Informational
When to Use	Before Reading, During Reading, After Reading
Comprehension Strategy	Determining Importance, Synthesizing
How to Use	Individual, Partner, Small Group, Whole Group

Description

The Venn diagram consists of two or more overlapping circles. It helps students organize information in a visual way. Through the use of a Venn Diagram, students can compare and contrast two or more ideas, themes, characters, or issues being studied. When the Venn is completed, students may create a written summary of the major relationships. By using a Venn Diagram, students can organize and evaluate information and then use the completed diagram as a vehicle for writing. Venn Diagrams can also be used before reading to make predictions about text.

Teaching Goals Related to Learner Outcomes

1. To help students organize information.
2. To help students make comparisons and contrasts among two or more topics.
3. To help students summarize information.

Procedure

1. Select one or more books, book chapters, major concepts, or a film and a book that you wish students to read and/or view.

2. When students have finished reading, listening to, or viewing the information, choose a topic and invite students to consider the similarities and differences in the information presented about the topic. For example, students may have read about orangutans (Lambeth, 2010) and chimpanzees (Schleichert, 2010) in classroom magazines. You might say the following.

    We have just read about two kinds of apes that live in other parts of the world. Let's consider some of the ways these apes are alike and also how they differ.

3. Distribute copies of a two-topic Venn Diagram (see page 108) or draw a Venn Diagram to be viewed by the entire group. Model how to use the reproducible using the example on page 107.

4. Write *Chimpanzees* on the line above one of the circles and *Orangutans* on the line above the other circle.

5. Explain to students that they should think about what they know about both of these animals that was confirmed from their reading or viewing. If an idea is true for both chimpanzees and orangutans, they should write the idea in the center where the two circles overlap. Ideas that relate to either animal, but not both, should be written under the appropriate headings. For example you might say the following.

    In our reading today, we learned that chimpanzees and orangutans are both intelligent animals. Let's list this idea in the center of our diagram where we put the ideas that are the same for both chimpanzees and orangutans. However, we also learned that orangutans are larger. We should list this fact in the circle under *Orangutans*.

6. Invite students to work to complete their Venn Diagrams, using the information from their text. You may wish to do one or two more examples with the group until you are confident that they understand how to proceed on their own in subsequent lessons.

7. When students have completed their diagrams, ask them to look at the information they have recorded on their diagrams and summarize verbally or in writing how chimpanzees are like orangutans. Then ask them to explain how they differ.

References

Lambeth, E. (2010, February). Life in the trees is a breeze. *Ranger Rick, 44*(2), 32–39.

Schleichert, E. (2010). Chimps are champs. *Ranger Rick, 44*(5), 5–10.

Venn Diagram

Chimpanzees

Orangutans

Different
- Live in Africa
- Black hair
- Live in groups
- Facial expressions show emotions
- 110-115 pounds

Alike
- Live in tropical rainforests
- Groom each other
- Have thumbs
- Intelligent
- Apes
- Laugh
- Endangered

Different
- Live in Borneo and Sumatra
- Reddish-brown hair
- Live in trees
- Live mostly alone
- 110-200 pounds

Name _____ Date _____

Venn Diagram

Different

Alike

Different

Name _____

Date _____

Venn Diagram

Name _____ Date _____

3-Way Venn Diagram

Topic/Concept: _____

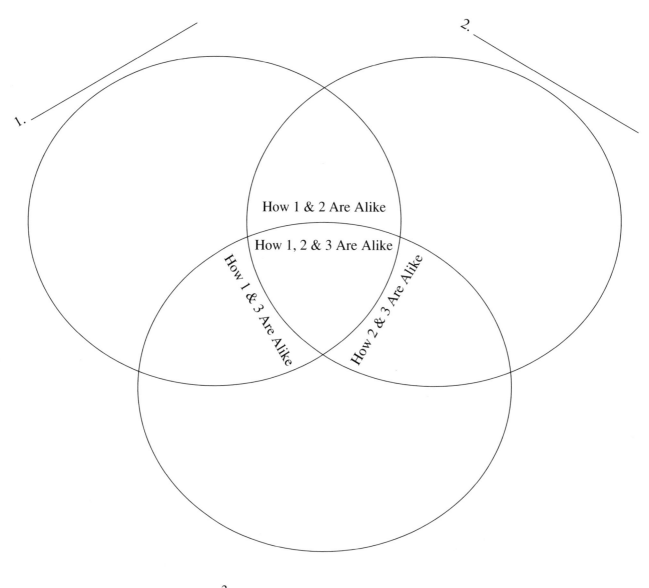

1.

2.

How 1 & 2 Are Alike

How 1, 2 & 3 Are Alike

How 1 & 3 Are Alike

How 2 & 3 Are Alike

3. _____

Conclusion

_____

_____

_____

Name _____ Date _____

3-Way Venn Diagram

Topic/Concept: _____

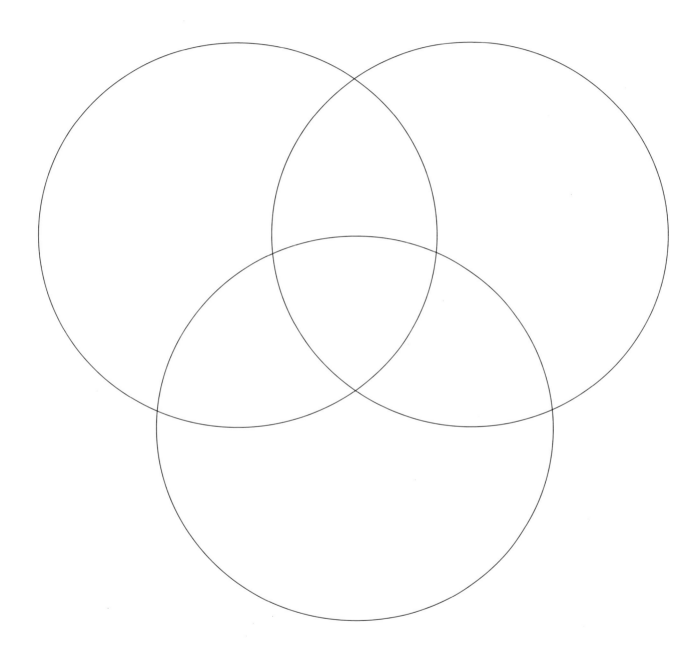

Name _____ Date _____

Venn Diagram

Topic/Concept: _____

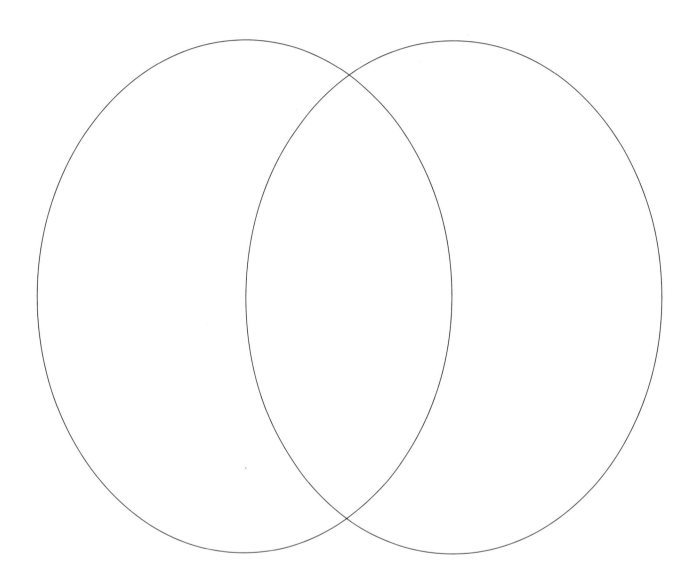

Conclusions/Connections/Questions/Realizations

Word Sorts

Text Type	Narrative, Informational
When to Use	Before Reading, During Reading, After Reading
Comprehension Strategy	Monitoring Meaning, Using Prior Knowledge, Asking Questions, Synthesizing
How to Use	Individual, Partner, Small Group, Whole Group

Description

Sorting words (Johns & Berglund, 2011) is a simple classification strategy that helps students organize and remember concepts (Gillet & Kita, 1979). Given a list of words, students are invited to consider the meaning or properties of each word and then sort the words into groups. There are two types of Word Sorts: Closed and Open. In a Closed Word Sort, students are given the categories and are then asked to place each word in one of the categories. In Open Word Sorts, students are given a collection of words and are asked to arrange them into groups, based on common features or categories determined by the students. Some of the words may become category headings or students can create new headings. Sorting words before reading can encourage predictions about the content. If used during and after reading they help to consolidate learning and clarify misconceptions.

Teaching Goals Related to Learner Outcomes

1. To help students become actively engaged in thinking about key words or concepts in a lesson.
2. To encourage students to engage in critical and inferential thinking.
3. To prompt divergent thinking and discussion.
4. To determine relationships between and among words or concepts.

Procedure

1. Select between 10 and 20 words that represent key concepts in a selection.
2. Copy the words onto cards, creating a set of cards for each group of 2–5 students.
3. Distribute the word cards to the students. If it is a Closed Sort, provide the category headings for the students. For an Open Sort, explain to students that it is their responsibility to determine how the words can be grouped together. It is important to emphasize that there may be several ways to organize the words. Students need to be able to explain the rationale for their decisions.
4. Give students 10–15 minutes to complete the sorts.
5. Conduct a class discussion regarding the students' grouping decisions.
6. If used as a pre-reading activity, invite students to return to their sorts after reading and reclassify words based on new understanding.

References

Gillet, J., & Kita, M. J. (1979). Words, kids and categories. *The Reading Teacher, 32*, 538–542.

Johns, J. L., & Berglund, R. L. (2011). *Strategies for content area learning* (3rd ed.). Dubuque, IA: Kendall Hunt.

Closed Word Sort Example

Categories Supplied by the Teacher: Reptiles   Non-Reptiles

Words

lizards snakes crocodiles parrots frogs toads panthers hawks dolphins
alligators manatees geckos pelicans seahorses chimpanzees orangutans

Sample of Student Work

Reptiles	Non-Reptiles
lizards	parrots
snakes	panthers
crocodiles	hawks
frogs	dolphins
alligators	manatees
geckos	pelicans
toads	seahorses
	chimpanzees
	orangutans

Open Word Sort Example

Words

lizards snakes crocodiles parrots frogs toads panthers hawks dolphins
alligators manatees geckos pelicans seahorses chimpanzees orangutans

Sample of Student Work

Three Categories Determined by One Group of Students

Live in Water	Live on Land	Live in Water and on Land
dolphins	lizards	snakes
manatees	parrots	crocodiles
seahorses	toads	frogs
	panthers	alligators
	hawks	
	geckos	
	pelicans	
	chimpanzees	
	orangutans	

Name _____ Date _____

Word Sort Cards

_____
Title and Author
